REMEMBERING WORLD WAR I

REMEMBERING WORLD WAR I:
An Engineer's Diary of the War

WRITTEN BY

Charles Edward Dilkes

1887 – 1968

EDITED BY

Virginia A. Dilkes

Georgia Dilkes Harris

Lola Dilkes Koniuszy

Juliet Publishing | Atlanta | 2014

Published by Juliet Publishing, Atlanta, Georgia
Published in the United States of America

ISBN 978 0 692 02861 2
Printed in the United States of America
First Edition: 2014

CONTENTS

Living History vi

List of Figures vii

Acknowledgements ix

Preface xi

Record of Military Service xiv

Pre-World War.. xviii

Dedication xix

Prologue xx

DIARY OF THE WAR 1

Chapter I: Washington, D.C., to St. Nazaire 2

Chapter II: St. Nazaire to Lunéville 10

FACING GERMAN SOLDIERS.. 15

Chapter III: Lunéville-Sommerviller Sector 16

Chapter IV: Toul-Ansauville Sector 22

Chapter V: The Storming of Cantigny 44

Chapter VI: Aisne-Marne Campaign... 74

THE WAR DIARY IN PICTURES 85

Chapter VII: Toul-Saizerais Sector 86

THE U.S. ARMY TAKES COMMAND 89

Chapter VIII: St. Mihiel Drive 90

Chapter IX: Meuse-Argonne Operation 102

Chapter X: Sedan... 112

Chapter XI: U.S. Army of Occupation in Germany..................... 124

Postscript 141

Appendix.. 145

Register of Notes 173

Glossary... 180

Bibliography... 183

Index 188

LIVING HISTORY

Reasons for the Entry of the United States into the World War xxiv

Organization and Movement Overseas: May 24 – December 22, 1917 8

1st Division Begins Training in Trenches 14

Relief of Ansauville Sector.. 26

Assembly of Units 1st Division Upon Relief... 32

Ansauville Sector 43

General Situation on 1st Division Front [May 13, 1918] 48

Cantigny Affair Emphasizes Importance of Organizing Our Own Divisions 63

Organization of Meuse-Argonne Operation 94

American Operations in the Meuse-Argonne Region: October 8, 1918 111

American Operations in the Meuse-Argonne Region: November 7, 1918 116

Advance of the 1st Division Toward Germany 122

Activities of Army of Occupation: May 1919... 135

Activities of Army of Occupation: December 19, 1918 – July 2, 1919.................. 137

Corps of 1st Engineers in World War I.. 138

LIST OF FIGURES

1. Sergeant Charles Edward Dilkes - 1918 xiv
2. Enlistment Record xv
3. Record of Military Service.. xvi
4. Membership in the Society of the First Division xvii
5. Map of Europe 1914: Before World War I xviii
6. Western Front in 1917 (Prior to U.S. Involvement) 2
7. Map of France: St. Nazaire to Lunéville.. 10
8. Map of Lunéville and Sommerviller Sector.. 16
9. Map of Ansauville Sector 22
10. Letter from Crédit Lyonnais Bank 37
11. Map of Battle for Cantigny 44
12. Map of Aisne-Marne (Soissons) Campaign.. 74
13. General Order 318.. 78
14. Map of St. Mihiel: Plan of Attack... 90
15. Map of St. Mihiel: 1st Division Positions.. 97
16. Map of the Meuse-Argonne Campaign: Phase 2 102
17. Map of the Meuse-Argonne Campaign: Oct. 7–10 107
18. Map of Battle for Sedan 112
19. Map of Armistice and the German Army Retreating.. 119
20. Zone of the American Army of Occupation... 124
21. Cartoon of History of the 1st Division in World War I 129
22. American Soldiers' & Sailors' Club Card.. 132
23. Farewell from General Pershing.. 139
24. Honorable Discharge 140
25. Map of Europe 1919: Post World War I.. 144
26. U.S. Army History of the Montdidier-Noyon Campaign.................................... 152
27. U.S. Army History of the Aisne-Marne Campaign 157
28. U.S. Army History of the St. Mihiel Campaign... 162
29. U.S. Army History of the Meuse-Argonne Campaign 171

ACKNOWLEDGEMENTS

The publication of the World War I memoirs of Charles Edward Dilkes has been a collaborative effort of the editors: Virginia Dilkes, Georgia Dilkes Harris, and Lola Dilkes Koniuszy, who are his daughters. We edited and reviewed his manuscript. We spent hours in libraries relating our father's memoirs to the written history of the War.

In publishing our father's memoirs, we included figures and notes to keep true to, and help explain, the culture and social fabric of that time in American history. When practical we used stylistic grammar from that period and 1910 – 1920 reference books including *Webster's New International Dictionary with Reference History*, published in 1910; *Americana* encyclopedia, published in 1912; and *Rand McNally New Reference Atlas of the World and the War*, published in 1918. We incorporated into this book our father's diary, his memoirs, his military record with military history, artifacts, the culture of trench warfare, the culture of American society, and current events of that time.

Attention to geographic detail was difficult because some names of the towns were phonetically spelled in the diary and some towns had more than one name depending on what country was the occupier. Despite these obstacles detailed maps of the military campaigns made it easy for us to follow the movements of our father during the War.

When we started this project, the intent was to document our father's contribution to the history of our country for our family's posterity: the ink was fading on his memoirs, the diary pages were becoming fragile, and the significance of the artifacts was beginning to be lost on the youngest generation. As the project progressed and nationwide media drew attention to the centennial anniversary of the First World War, people outside of our family expressed interest in what we were doing. It became clear we needed to broaden the audience for the book. We wanted to share our father's story with others who have had loved ones involved in the First World War. Some of the endnotes and words in the glossary will seem trivial to the older generations, but our focus is on telling the story of our father for the generations to come.

We would like to thank members of Charles Edward Dilkes' family for their contributions to the publication of these memoirs with a special note of appreciation to Mrs. Charles E. (Mary) Dilkes, his wife and our mother, who kept alive the memory of our father's WWI service to our country; she preserved his WWI memoirs and passed them on to us. Our sister, Mary Dilkes Bangert, and her family helped with style. Our brothers, Charles E. Dilkes, Jr., and Harry Dilkes, provided us with many of the artifacts. Anne Dunning offered document guidance, and Jim Dunning, Jr., worked with us on technology. Jim Bell Harris' enthusiasm for this book was greatly appreciated along with his support from a historical perspective. We would like to thank the staff at the National Archives who helped us with the maps of the 1st Division military campaigns, which showed the location of Camp Essayons, and assisted us with the picture on our book cover. Mike Hanlon, editor of World War I periodicals including the *St. Mihiel Trip-Wire* and *Over the Top*, and editor of the daily blog *Roads to the Great War*, directed us to several World War I resources used to document our father's experiences. Jonathan Casey, Archivist for the National World War I Museum, provided us with a copy of the book *A History of the 1st U.S. Engineers* that included our father's name. We are grateful for the comments offered by members of the World War One Historical Association. A special thank-you goes to David Laufer who has worked with us in various capacities including graphic artist, designer, and advisor, and who has never ceased to extend his support.

PREFACE

Charles Edward Dilkes was an engineer-soldier in World War I. Prior to volunteering to help in the war effort, he had pursued engineering studies at Holy Cross College. He transferred to Georgetown University from where he graduated in 1910. When the United States declared war on Germany in 1917, he answered the call to duty and joined a company of engineers. He served as a volunteer in the 1st Division, and as an engineer his job was to construct fortifications, prepare the terrain for battle, pick up arms when ordered, and repair damage done by battle. He was often under attack while performing these tasks, and as such he was able to eye the War from the front lines of many of the major battles on the Western Front.

Charles Edward Dilkes is our father. He was a wise man, a good and gentle person, quite formal yet entertaining, and very patriotic. He was religious and never used maledictions, as he referred to obscenities. Like many veterans who fought at the front lines, he did not like to talk about the War unless asked. After the War he became an inventor who went on to build a business in the printing industry.

He saved many artifacts from his World War I service to our country and from that period in American history: his Enlistment and Discharge papers; General Orders; a Crédit Lyonnais Bank correspondence responding to his letter requesting the bank return a money draft to his father in his failed attempt to exchange the draft for currency in France; a "Strange As It Seems" cartoon about the First Division; his sister's calling card from the American Soldiers' & Sailors' Club in Paris where he and his sister, Marie-Louise, met while on leave after the hostilities ceased; commendations extolling the accomplishments of the 1st Division; and a newspaper dated

November 11, 1918, proclaiming the armistice[1] that ended the War. We validated the artifacts when possible and wrote letters to identified sources. In some cases the sources responded; in other cases no response was received. We continue to seek information on the sources related to the artifacts.

Our father realized the War was going to be a significant part of American history, and he wanted to document his experience. He kept a daily diary from the day he left training camp in 1917 to embark on his journey to fight in the War in Europe until the day in 1919 when he was granted a pass to go to Paris to visit his sister. At one point in his memoirs, in his recollection of the Aisne-Marne Campaign, he wrote that he buried his diary alongside his trench in fear the Germans would discover it if the German attack was successful; under cover of darkness he was able to retrieve these notes. When he returned home, he wrote his memoirs of the Great War based on his diary and his recollections of his experiences as an engineer-soldier and conversations he had with other soldiers in the field. His stories and our memory of him will live with us.

Charles Edward Dilkes died in 1968. He left us his memoirs, his diary, and his artifacts, which we would like to share with you. His memoirs, written in the style of the early 1900s, reflect his thoughts and actions as a soldier from his patriotic call to duty, to his experiences during the war, to his desire to return to civilian life. We included photographs he kept of the War. Some of the photographs are disturbing, as death is neither pleasing to record nor pleasant to look at.

To complement our father's memoirs, we have included several historical records from the U.S. Army Center of Military History. We titled these selective records "Living History," which relate our country's documented history to our father's experiences and account of the War. These historical records underscore the contribution the engineers of the First Division made to the successful outcome of the War.

You will read throughout these memoirs how literature influenced our father's life. The best-known poem from World War I is "In Flanders Fields" by John McCrae.[2] We include "In Flanders Fields" in memory of our father who lived to write about the War and in memory of the soldiers who gave their lives so that we may live ours.

"In Flanders Fields"

In Flanders fields the poppies blow
Between the crosses, row on row
That mark our place; and in the sky
The larks, still bravely singing, fly
Scarce heard amid the guns below.

We are the Dead. Short days ago
We lived, felt dawn, saw sunset glow,
Loved and were loved, and now we lie
In Flanders fields.

Take up our quarrel with the foe:
To you from failing hands we throw
The torch; be yours to hold it high.
If ye break faith with us who die
We shall not sleep, though poppies grow
In Flanders fields.

Figure 1: Sergeant Charles Edward Dilkes - 1918

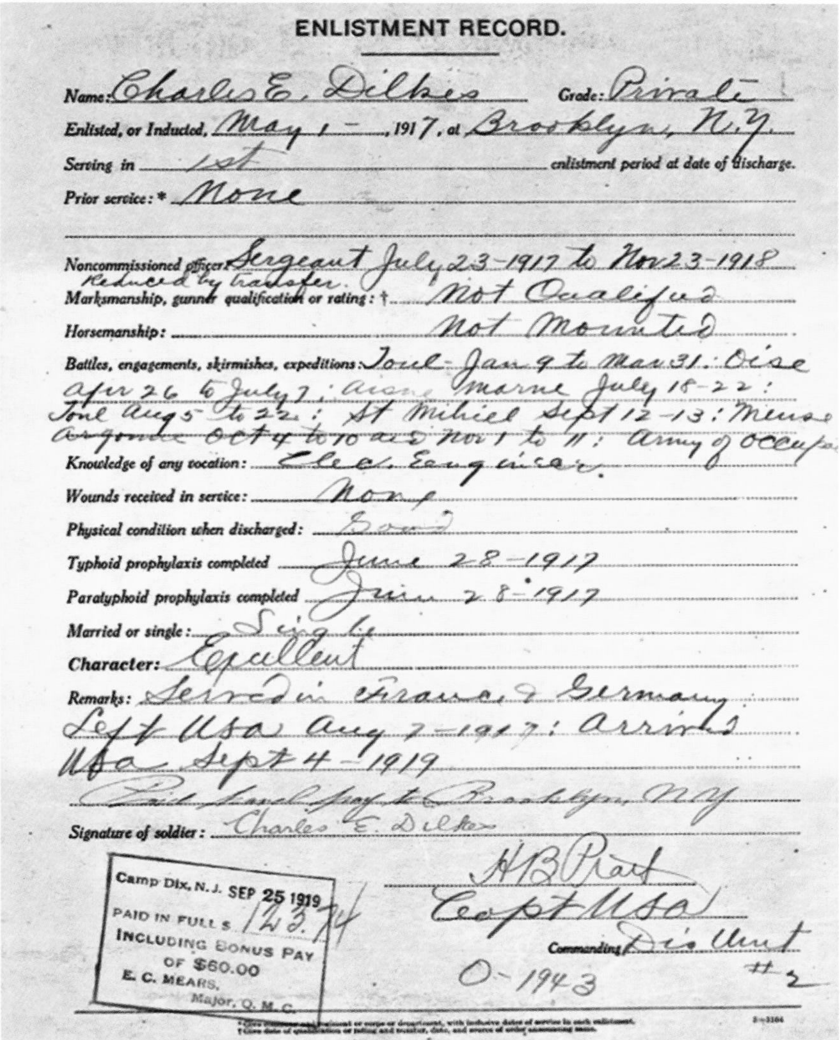

ENLISTMENT RECORD.

Name: *Charles E. Dilkes*   Grade: *Private*

Enlisted, or Inducted, *May 1* — , 1917, at *Brooklyn, N.Y.*

Serving in *1st* _____ enlistment period at date of discharge.

Prior service: * *None*

Noncommissioned officer *Sergeant July 23-1917 to Nov 23-1918*
Reduced by transfer.
Marksmanship, gunner qualification or rating: † *Not Qualified*

Horsemanship: *Not Mounted*

Battles, engagements, skirmishes, expeditions: *Toul-Jan 9 to Mar 31: Oise*
Aisne 26 to July 7: Aisne Marne July 18-22:
Toul Aug 5 to 22: St Mihiel Sept 12-13: Meuse
Argonne Oct 4 to 10 and Nov 1 to 11: Army of Occupa

Knowledge of any vocation: *Elec Engineer.*

Wounds received in service: *None*

Physical condition when discharged: *Good*

Typhoid prophylaxis completed *June 28-1917*

Paratyphoid prophylaxis completed *June 28-1917*

Married or single: *Single*

Character: *Excellent*

Remarks: *Served in France & Germany*
Left USA Aug 7-1917: Arrived
USA Sept 4-1919
Paid final pay to Brooklyn, N.Y.

Signature of soldier: *Charles E. Dilkes*

Camp Dix, N.J. SEP 25 1919
PAID IN FULL $ *143.74*
INCLUDING BONUS PAY
OF $60.00
E. C. MEARS.
Major, Q.M.C.

H B Pratt
Capt USA
Commanding *Dis Unit*
#2
O-1943

Figure 2: Enlistment Record

RECORD OF MILITARY SERVICE

U.S. Army	1st Division: May 1, 1917 – September 25, 1919
Company F	1st Engineers: May 1917 – December 1918
Company E	1st Engineers: Jan. 1919 – September 1919

May 1, 1917	Enlisted in U.S. Army; assigned to Company F
August 7, 1917	Disembarked for active duty in World War I
January 2, 1918	Submitted name for Officers' Training Corps
January 18, 1918	Named acting sergeant[3]
April 2, 1918	Promoted to sergeant
June 9 – 13, 1918	Awarded Victory Medal for Cantigny / Montdidier-Noyon Campaign
July 18 – Aug. 6, 1918	Awarded Victory Medal for Aisne-Marne Campaign
Sep. 12 – 16, 1918	Awarded Victory Medal for St. Mihiel Campaign
Sep. 26 – Nov.11, 1918	Awarded Victory Medal for Meuse-Argonne Campaign
December 16, 1918	Transferred to Company E; wartime rank reduced to peacetime rank[4]
September 4, 1919	Arrived home from World War I
September 25, 1919	Received honorable discharge

Figure 3: Record of Military Service

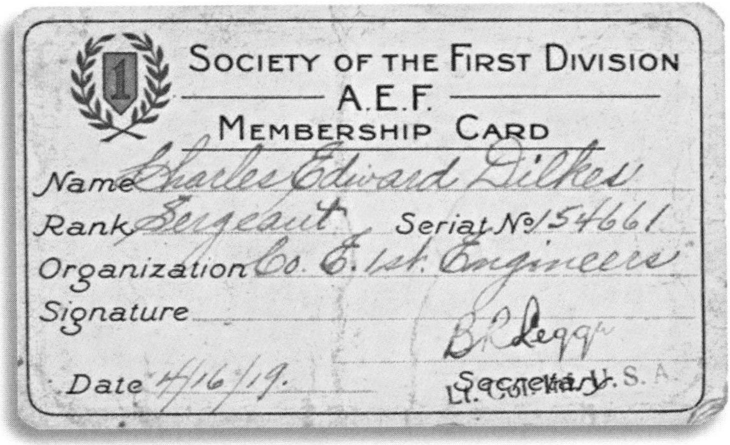

SOCIETY OF THE FIRST DIVISION
——— A.E.F. ———
MEMBERSHIP CARD

Name *Charles Edward Dilkes*
Rank *Sergeant* Serial No *154661*
Organization *Co. E. 1st. Engineers*
Signature

B R Legg

Date *4/16/19.* Lt. Secretary. U.S.A.

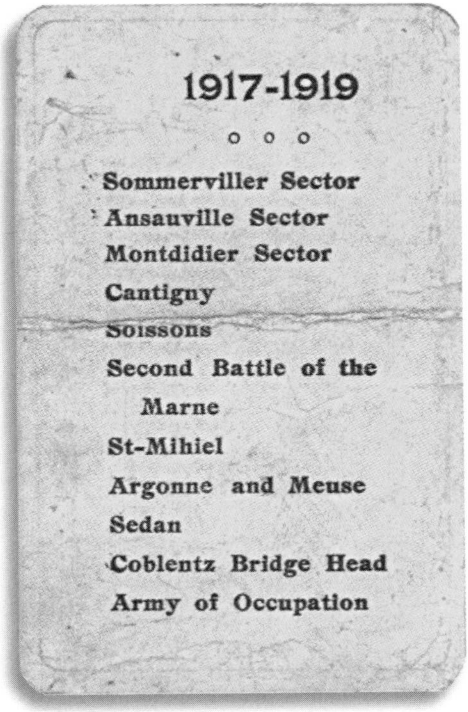

1917-1919

o o o

Sommerviller Sector
Ansauville Sector
Montdidier Sector
Cantigny
Soissons
Second Battle of the
Marne
St-Mihiel
Argonne and Meuse
Sedan
Coblentz Bridge Head
Army of Occupation

Figure 4: Membership in the Society of the First Division
(Sector Service Record)[5]

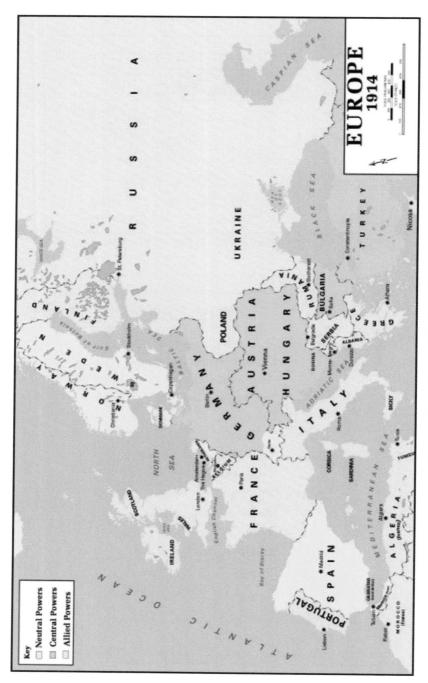

Figure 5: Map of Europe 1914: Before World War I [6]

DEDICATION

To my father whose anxiety, kindness and thoughtfulness were never lacking ...

To my mother whose prayers, gifts and letters of encouragement helped bolster up my spirits during the darkest moments ...

To my sister, Louise, whose earnest efforts while engaged in war work carried this insight to the very front lines ...

To my brother, Jim ...

To my brothers and sisters whose gracious assistance during this bitter campaign lightened my burden when discouraged and depressed ...

To all
I express my deepest gratitude and profound thanks for their kindness ...

To all my friends whose thoughts were greatly accentuated by their acts, to them I pour my heart out to and thank them ... .

Charles E. Dilkes

PROLOGUE

There are various statements given and various opinions formed as to why the thousands volunteered at the outbreak of our great conflict with Germany.

In setting forth my reasons for joining the colors, no doubt the same reasons can be attributed to others, for it soon became evident that every man must shoulder a weapon in defense of his home.

At first America's entrance into the conflict appeared to some to be unwarranted, foolish, and an act of infringement. Even now with the signing of the armistice and peace, there are many who feel it was a needless waste of money and lives. It was our only alternative. Even admitting the great sacrifice of 7,990,000 lives and 18,000,000 wounded, I still was ready and willing to be numbered among these to prevent a disaster to my country as befell France, and still there are many who wonder why such a slaughter should be, and what it was all about. Very appropriate is the following verse, but I assure you it was much different.

"After Blenheim"[7]

It was a summer evening,
Old Kaspar's work was done,
And he before his cottage door
Was sitting in the sun;
And by him sported on the green
His little grandchild Wilhelmine.

She saw her brother Peterkin
Roll something large and round
Which he beside the rivulet
In playing there had found;
He came to ask what he had found
That was so large and smooth and round.

Old Kaspar took it from the boy,
Who stood expectant by;
And then the old man shook his head,
And with a natural sigh,
"'Tis some poor fellow's skull," said he,
"Who fell in the great victory.

"I find them in the garden,
For there's many here about;
And often, when I go to plough,
The ploughshare turns them out;
For many thousand men," said he,
"Were slain in that great victory."

"Now tell us what 'twas all about,"
Young Peterkin he cries;
And little Wilhelmine looks up
With wonder-waiting eyes;
"Now tell us all about the war,
And what they fought each other for."

"It was the English," Kaspar cried,
"Who put the French to rout;
But what they fought each other for
I could not well make out.
But everybody said," quoth he,
"That 'twas a famous victory.

"My father lived at Blenheim then,
Yon little stream hard by;
They burnt his dwelling to the ground,
And he was forced to fly:
So with his wife and child he fled,
Nor had he where to rest his head.

"With fire and sword the country round
Was wasted far and wide,
And many a childing mother then
And newborn baby died;
But things like that, you know, must be
At every famous victory.

"They say it was a shocking sight
After the field was won;
For many thousand bodies here
Lay rotting in the sun;
But things like that, you know, must be
After a famous victory.

"Great praise the Duke of Marlbro' won,
And our good Prince Eugene."
"Why, 'twas a very wicked thing!"
Said little Wilhelmine.
"Nay—nay—my little girl," quoth he,
"It was a famous victory.

"And everybody praised the Duke
Who this great fight did win."
"But what good came of it at last?"
Quoth little Peterkin.
"Why that I cannot tell," said he,
"But 'twas a famous victory."

I saw but one reason for Germany wishing to combat nations, not a nation but nations, for she well knew that it was impossible to wage conflict with one nation without the intervention of another.

With the aid of Austria-Hungary[8] she was now ready to strike and strike hard and crush, with a Teutonic[9] plague, all nations till the seed of victory was planted in the middle of the Atlantic and till she waved the flag of Germany in glory and acclaimed her nation as ruler of the world.

This bold assertion was emphasized to all nations in August of the year 1914 by a deadly rain of shellfire upon the astounding but still peaceful Frenchmen. Germany felt confident in subduing England and France with tremendous slaughter on the Western Front,[10] while Russia was gradually being brought to her knees. Austria was overwhelming Italy. However the big mistake, the grave error of the forty years of preparedness,[11] was Germany's utter disregard for the United States, but her chief concern now.

To relieve the situation in America, Germany's other army, and more deadly than her fighting forces in Europe, was thrown with full force and impetus against the unprepared forces of the United States. Spies, intrigues, conspirators, and bomb plotters ran rampant throughout our country plotting and scheming to embroil the United States in some conflict at home. Her main weapon was Mexico, and it was to this country, mind you, Germany promised the states of Arizona and Texas, if Mexico would take up arms against America and ally herself with Germany.

Just to think, this audacious proposal was made by a foreign country, and this foreign country offered to give something which it did not possess. What did this mean? Keep America fighting in America and we will be on to help you. This proposal was justified on Germany's part since she well knew the rich resources of the United States. Was not America her goal?

Well for three years up to this point Germany was hammering at the gates of Paris, leaving a trail of dead and dying behind her, laying waste village after village, murdering, pillaging, and driving into slavery the French and English. For three years our country was aware of the frightfulness on the seas: ships sunk at will until a shout of protest and defiance resounded to the very dome of the Imperial Castle.[12] So on the 6th of April 1917, from continent to continent, traveled the vital word that America was to mobilize:

WAR WAS DECLARED AGAINST GERMANY.

Living History

REASONS FOR THE ENTRY OF THE UNITED STATES INTO THE WORLD WAR[13]

Events which drove the United States into war developed rapidly. On February 26, 1917, the President requested Congress to give him authority to equip American merchant ships with defensive arms should that become necessary. Two days later the President gave to the press the contents of a telegram which had been intercepted by the British Government late in January. This telegram had been sent by the German Secretary of Foreign Affairs, Arthur Zimmermann, through the German Embassy in Washington to the German Minister in Mexico City. It proposed that, in the event of war between the United States and Germany, an alliance be formed between Mexico and Germany and that Mexico endeavor to persuade Japan to desert the Allies and align herself with the Central Powers. Mexico was to be allowed "to reconquer her lost territory in Texas, New Mexico and Arizona." The effect of the publication of this telegram seemed to crystallize public opinion into a strong furling of hostility toward Germany.

After the sinking of American ships by German submarines had actually occurred, the President addressed a special session of Congress on April 2, 1917, saying that under Germany's new policy "Vessels of every kind, whatever their flag, their character, their cargo, their destination, their errand, have been ruthlessly sent to the bottom without warning and without thought of help or mercy for those on board, the vessels of friendly neutrals along with those of belligerents. Even hospital ships and ships carrying relief to the sorely bereaved and stricken people of Belgium ... have been sunk with the same reckless lack of compassion and of principle." He further stated that he was not "thinking of the loss of property, immense and serious as that is, but only of the wanton and wholesale destruction of the lives of non-combatants, men, women, and children engaged in pursuits which have always, even in the darkest periods of modern history, been deemed innocent and legitimate...." He then advised that war be declared against the Imperial German Government. Congress, with but few dissenting votes, approved this recommendation and war was declared against Germany on April 6, 1917.

United States Army Center of Military History (1998), "The World War to May 28, 1918 and the Organization of the American Expeditionary Force," United States Army in World War I, version 2, CD-ROM disc 3 of 3: 11.

DIARY OF THE WAR

1917-1919

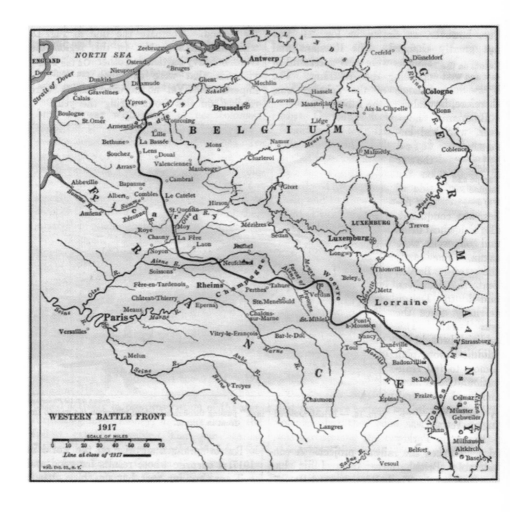

Figure 6: Western Front in 1917
(Prior to U.S. Involvement)[14]

I

WASHINGTON, D.C., TO ST. NAZAIRE

If someone in the year 1916 told me in the year 1917 that I would be in the Army, it would have been a word of insanity. However, it is just what happened. I with hundreds of others boasted of supreme patriotism and answered Uncle Sam's call on the 1st of May. After the distribution process, I found myself doing duty as a private in the Engineers at Washington Barracks, Washington, D.C. The course of instructions, new in its entirety to anything I had yet experienced, found me responding quite readily. I quickly adapted myself to all conditions then in vogue. Three months of a daily routine of drills, inspections, reviews, and hikes were sufficient to have us wonder if the War existed or not. Our very beings began to hanker for the trip across. We craved for some more definite activity towards our goal. It came and events followed. Everything was packed. "Barracks for rent—unfurnished" would have been an appropriate sign to hang outside the barracks. Where all this equipment was going, no one knew.

For two days we remained at the barracks with nothing but our packs to offer the best comforts possible under the circumstances. No letters acquainting our families of this sudden departure were written. The absolute ignorance of our movements that we all experienced was surely remarkable, for there was no knowledge indicative of our destination that could be withheld. No one could leave the barracks without special permission. Profound secrecy was insisted upon. The preparations which were completed at this early stage became very interesting. Any news informed to the enemy would have greatly embarrassed the Command and perhaps caused great disaster, owing to the inexperience of our country in transporting troops abroad.

However, any dissatisfaction at events leading up to this one night, the night of departure, was completely assuaged by the inspiring attitude and effect of the regimental band. I wish you could share my anticipation with me when on August 6, 1917, at 6:30 p.m., all men were assembled with full field equipment; and at 7:00 p.m. we marched through the huge iron gates, thronged with people waving their last good-byes to the First Engineers.[15] Each Company marched out singly. The band preceding the first Company escorted it to the gate and, by a well-directed movement, disengaged itself, allowing this first Company to proceed, followed now by the spirited strains of "Over There." The band now stationed at the entrance greeted each Company in turn as it marched up the road and out, accentuating the enormousness of the occasion with its untiring playing in expression of encouragement. The first emotion of the War was experienced at home.

Full of spirit and hope we boarded the troop train at 8:30 p.m. We spent a restless night, but I can't say a weary journey, for card playing, singing, and music were much in evidence throughout the trip. Early on the morning of the 7th the trains arrived in Jersey City, New Jersey, where we boarded the ferry for Hoboken, New Jersey, where the transport *Finland*[16] lay. With but little confusion at 11:00 a.m., the regiment with two hundred nurses and two Base Hospital Units was safely on board and bunks assigned. Once everyone was concealed in the hold of the ship, at 12:30 p.m. the *Finland* dropped down the bay off Tomkinsville, New York. Here we stayed at anchor till 8:00 p.m. when the issuing of orders and throbbing of engines acquainted us with our departure from the shores of America. Soon we were all up on deck for all our movements were now covered by darkness. There was but little to see so the slogan "early to bed" was adopted ... and this night the long trip to France began.

I arose with the sun next morning, August 8th, and from the confinement of the day before was glad to get up on deck and view things unhampered. The excitement of the last few days was awakened once more when I beheld our small fleet of ships consisting of five transports, each carrying its quota of troops, three submarine chasers, and the battleship *Texas*. As my vigil increased, also did my interest in the continuous maneuvering of the fleet: first in line, then abreast, battle formation, then skirmish fashion, orders signaled from one ship to another—all bore a marked contrast to what was experienced on land. As my ship was the commanding boat, all orders were taken and received from it. Hence, the movements of all vessels were expected and watched with much interest.

Our days were strenuously devoted to boat drills, lectures on the operation of lifeboats, and procedures to follow when in an attack or in case we needed to abandon ship. Orders were very rigid regarding the behavior on entering the lifeboats, with each assigned to his or her boat and any disobedience of commands to be dealt with by means of a pistol. Calisthenics were also held daily while amusements of various sorts helped relieve the monotony of our sailor life. The programs of the day included boxing, wrestling, performing vaudeville acts, piano playing, and crap shooting. Arriving on deck the 10th of August, I was informed that the convoy had turned back in the night and traveled for five miles toward New York. I assumed this maneuver was to delay our entrance into the submarine zone in case the enemy became aware of the date of our departure.

On the 11th I was doing duty as submarine guard. Taking my post at the stern of the ship, my instructions were that anything suspicious floating in the water was to be reported. Nothing unusual marred the peacefulness of my watch, but I gladly welcomed the relief when it came. Other details, such as the crow's nest,[17] were worse. The crow's nest is a semi-cylindrical box located at the bow of the ship on top of the mast. Here you must be constantly on the alert observing everything and reporting all to the officer on watch by shouting out what is seen. A barrel, a box, wreckage, or anything seen by the eye in the water must be reported at the time of sighting.

On two occasions a ship was seen on the horizon, and immediately one of the destroyers sailed out to investigate to learn if it was of enemy stock or not. The precautions were well justified for submarine activity was a recognized fact. Any orange peelings, paper, or refuse of any kind thrown overboard was a court martial offense. Smoking on deck at night was a crime punishable by death. No lights were allowed that could be seen from without. At night with intense vigil, endeavoring to locate our transports, I would attempt to penetrate the darkness—but no sign of a ship could I see. On the 14th orders were issued that life belts be worn at all times. Boat drills also became more regular and instructions more emphatic.

On August 15, 1917, a heavy fog settled down during which one of our transports was lost out of sight of the convoy. We lost one hour of time before it appeared again in the distance on the horizon. There was a continuous gale blowing at this time in which we experienced our first rolling, but no one became sick. On August 17, 1917, about 800 miles from the French coast, five destroyers met us to convoy us to port. The battle cruiser *Texas* that had accompanied us up to this time was about to turn back for America with two destroyers. However, late in the afternoon the engine room crew of our steamer *Finland* refused to work. So before the battleship *Texas* left us, a crew from that ship was sent to replace our crew. It was interesting to watch the continual semaphore[18] signaling between the ships and the transfer of the crews in the smooth sea. We now had decreased protection, but nothing unusual happened.

The 18th of August found us well within the danger zone, and a most careful and rigid watch was exacted. By this time our imaginations were running rampant, everyone believing he could spy a periscope on the water. The next day a submarine was actually sighted at 2:30 in the afternoon. Our aft gun blazed away at her, probably missing, as there was no report of the outcome. On the 20th, as was my custom, about eight o'clock in the morning I was just coming on deck when a big explosion occurred, shaking the ship and causing much excitement. The Captain from the bridge shouted out, "Why the hell don't you shoot that submarine!" when immediately our fore gun blazed away, sending forth its deadly shell and causing everyone to climb on the masts and every available place to get a good view of what promised to be a most exciting encounter—a battle with the submarines.

There was a regular school of submarines within 100 to 200 yards of us. All our guns went into action against them; every ship in our convoy took battle formation with every boat for itself. The activities of the submarines seemed to be centered on the *Finland*. Our destroyers were skirting swiftly about dropping depth bombs, and our airplanes were flying everywhere, high and low, dropping to within five feet of the water, letting down their bombs when they sighted a submarine, a signal to all to let their guns go at the spot. This was the only action experienced by any American transport on its way "over there." The number of submarines was of course unknown, but on our side we had five armed transports, six destroyers, and two airplanes. It looked like a moving picture show; everyone, even the women nurses aboard, were calm yet interested in all the excitement. The battle raged for one and a half hours. Later we were told that we had sunk two U-boats. There was no damage to any of our ships. The news of the firing we learned afterwards reached St. Nazaire, 80 miles away, and a signal to them that a new convoy was arriving with American troops to aid in the cause of France and the world.

On the 20th of August at 4:30 in the afternoon, we dropped anchor in the beautiful harbor of St. Nazaire. The next day we landed amidst the shouts of welcome and joy of the French and Americans. We proceeded immediately to Camp No. 1, where we were quartered in French barracks, thus completing our long journey "over there" and our introduction to the Great War without loss of life.[19]

The period of which I shall now tell you is one of preparation and training, covering over seven months from August 21, 1917, to April 6, 1918.

Living History

ORGANIZATION AND MOVEMENT OVERSEAS:
MAY 24 – DECEMBER 22, 1917[20]

May 24, War Department directs organization of the First Expeditionary Division (later designated 1st Division), Regular Army. The majority of the troops selected are in service near the Mexican border at Brownsville, Douglas, El Paso, San Benito, and Fts Bliss, Ringgold, and Sam Houston; others are at Washington Barracks and Ft Oglethorpe; new organizations join at the ports of embarkation. June 3, the first contingent, consisting of the 16th, 18th, 26th, and 28th Regts of Inf, F Hosp 6 (later designated 13), Amb Co 6 (later designated 13), and Co C 2d F Sig Bn, after being increased to authorized strength by transfers and voluntary enlistments, moves to Hoboken. June 7, 2d Inf Brig, which includes the 26th and 28th Regts of Inf, is formed in New York City. June 8, Brig Gen William L. Sibert assumes command of the Div. June 9, 1st Inf Brig, which includes the 16th and 18th Regts of Inf, is formed in New York City. June 14, DHQ, Hq 1st Inf Brig, Hq 2d Inf Brig, and the first contingent sail from New York and Hoboken, and arrive June 26 at St. Nazaire. July 22, the second contingent, consisting of the 5th, 6th, and 7th Regts of FA, and Cos A and B 2d F Sig Bn begins the journey from Texas and Arizona to Hoboken, sails July 31 from Hoboken, and arrives Aug 13 at St. Nazaire. **Aug 6, 1st Engrs and Tn move from Washington Barracks to Hoboken, sail Aug 7, and arrive Aug 20 at St. Nazaire.** Aug 7, the Motor Bn of the Am Tn and 1st TM Btry sail from Hoboken and arrive Aug 21 at St. Nazaire. Aug 13, the Horse Bn of the Am Tn, F Hosps 2 and 12 and Amb Cos 2 and 12 of the 1st Sn Tn, and the 1st and 2d MP Cos sail from Hoboken, land Sept 1 and 3 at Liverpool, and after a short stay in rest camps move to Le Havre. Dec 1, F Hosp 3 leaves Ft Bliss, and Amb Co 3 Ft Oglethorpe, for Hoboken, sail Dec 5, and arrive Dec 22 at St. Nazaire, completing the overseas movement of the Division....

COMPLETION OF ORGANIZATION IN FRANCE
JULY 5, 1917 - FEBRUARY 17, 1918[21]

...August 21, Cos A and B 2d F Sig Bn arrive in Gondrecourt Area where they are joined by the Motor Bn Am Tn, F Hosps 2 and 10, Div trains with Fr 18th Div which replaces the Fr 47th Div (Chasseurs). During the winter the infantry units furnish the personnel for the 1st, 2d, and 3d MG Bns which are formed in the Gondrecourt Area. Feb 17, the 1st Sup Tn is organized in this area.

United States Army Center of Military History (1998). "Order of Battle of the United States Land Forces in the World War, American Expeditionary Forces Division," *United States Army in World War I*, version 2, CD-ROM disc 3 of 3, volume II: 5,7.

Figure 7: Map of France: St. Nazaire to Lunéville[22]

ST. NAZAIRE TO LUNÉVILLE

AUGUST 21 - OCTOBER 20, 1917

We remained at St. Nazaire for eleven days, busy policing the town and cleaning it up and making quarters. In the evenings most of us took advantage of permission to visit the city proper, sampling the wonderful French wines which were quite new to us. Increasing our conversational knowledge of the language, mostly learned through gestures, we managed to get along. It was always interesting walking back the three miles along the country roads to our camp. The population of St. Nazaire is about 5,000 inhabitants. It is a thriving business town with its chief industry being fisheries. The people are very friendly and frequently offered us their hospitality, inviting us to their houses for dinner and entertaining us generally in the gracious French way. We were also engaged during these days in drills of various kinds.

On August 27, 1917, we experienced a tremendous windstorm which tore things up, requiring a great deal of work on our part, especially to restore things to their original order. On the 30th we got our first glimpse of a batch of German prisoners who were engaged before we came in repairing the roads; and from them we heard their side of the war from a German point of view. At this time they were still confident that Germany would win and that it would be but a short time before France and England would be brought to their knees. Since we have as yet had no experience up at the firing line, we took what they said as probable truth. These Germans were very interesting fellows from the lowest walks of society,[23] and, of course, their concepts of the war were quite crude. They were mostly from the laboring class, although volunteers. We had two interesting days of experience in coaling ships in the harbor of St. Nazaire, with the rest of the time being engaged in repairing roads.

On the 1st of September we left St. Nazaire, entraining on box cars without springs. The box cars were marked *"40 hommes—8 chevaux."*[24] We were greeted vociferously all along the route especially by boys yelling "biscuits, cigarettes!" We had little sleep, but really enjoyed the beautiful scenery. Sleeping was done in relays, half of us sleeping for two hours while the other half stood up. On the 5th we arrived at Givrauval about 20 miles from the front. Givrauval had 200 inhabitants. We slept in barns and on straw. We cleaned up the streets. We cut firewood, a French native designating which trees we might cut down.

The people here never got news of the outside world in the regular way, but a town crier rang a bell and bawled the news in public. Meals were still cooked in the open fireplace. The church is the biggest structure in town, always picturesque. In fact every village in France has its own church, no matter how small the town. Around here we practiced ten-mile hikes. We could easily hear the firing ten miles away and see observation balloons. A series of events followed: I came down with ptomaine poisoning while doing guard duty, ran into a barbed wire[25] fence in the dark and got cut up, and at one point sat in a beehive.[26]

On September 11th we went to Bourmont, 60 miles away and 50 miles from the front. It was a pretty town on a high hill. We drank much wine and talked to the French girls, and despite the rain and mud we built barracks and hospitals. Here the men were attached to different French schools. I with ten others was chosen for the cantonment[27] school and sent to Harreville, a town of 150 people, reaching there on the 13th. There was a mix up in the order, as the French officers did not know anything about our mission. We were the first Americans to arrive in this town. On the first night here a party was arranged for us at which champagne flowed freely, and we had all kinds of entertainment. On the 20th we went to Landaville, a town of 100 people, to construct barracks. Here I met the French *curé*[28] who could speak very little English but picked up our lingo with surprising ease. We were quartered in a barn with the public cow.

On the 23rd we returned to Bourmont. One of the men got drunk, but before he would move from his position on the roadway, an officer had to threaten him with his pistol; he got five years in the penitentiary. We traded our clothes and laundry for the delicious French wine. Our first fatality occurred here from a fall off the back of a truck. We built barracks and stables and repaired the roads around the area. I raised a beard of two or three months' growth before I was ordered to take it off. I got my first letter from home on Monday, October 1, 1917, a memorable day for me. On the 8th I celebrated my birthday.

We received word on October 11th to get ready to leave for Gondrecourt, 30 miles away. It had been raining for nine straight days, and it was still raining when we left for Gondrecourt. On the 13th we left Gondrecourt for Abainville where we arrived on the 14th. The weather all this time was very cold with constant rain and of course mud. We established winter quarters in this town of 250 people and went into extensive training in trench digging, bayonet exercises, throwing hand grenades, and casting liquid fire.[29] None of these towns was permitted to show lights at night. While here I got another pile of letters from home and some literature. On the 17th at 9 a.m. we witnessed French anti-aircraft trying to bring down a German aviator. When these fellows flew around, the custom was to lie flat on one's face on the ground so as not to be seen. The German aviator hovered around for 20 minutes in the dark. We organized squads against air raids to signal their approach. We experienced many air raids here. On the 20th we were initiated into the mysteries of using gas masks.

Living History

1ST DIVISION BEGINS TRAINING IN TRENCHES[30]

HEADQUARTERS, A.E.F.,

No. 234S   Chaumont, Haute-Marne, October 20, 1917.

Agwar, Washington

For the Chief of Staff

The 1st Division will begin training in quiet portion of the trenches northeast of Lunéville on 20th. First group consisting of one battalion from each regiment of infantry will remain ten days followed by similar groups of four battalions each for like periods. Artillery will generally reinforce the French artillery behind trenches occupied by our Infantry. Quiet section has been selected and actual lines will be occupied by alternate companies or double companies of French and American troops. Every precaution will be taken to prevent anything serious happening but such experience in trenches deemed very necessary and follows French practice. Upon completion of the thirty days necessary for the entire division, the infantry and artillery [of the] 1st Division will train together according to prescribed program extending to about February 1. Other divisions according to progress will be sent to trenches for short periods in same manner.

PERSHING.

United States Army Center of Military History (1998), "Training and Use of American Units with the British and French," *United States Army in World War I,* version 2, CD-ROM disc 1 of 3, volume III: 449.

FACING GERMAN SOLDIERS

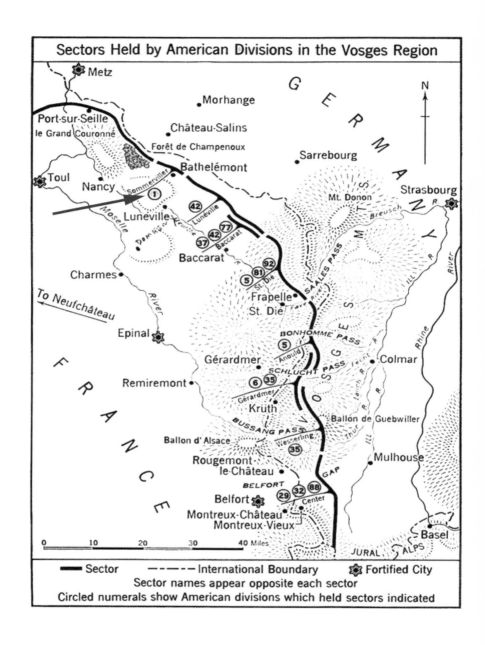

Figure 8: Map of Lunéville and Sommerviller Sector[31]

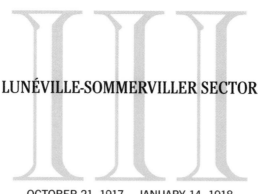

LUNÉVILLE-SOMMERVILLER SECTOR

OCTOBER 21, 1917 – JANUARY 14, 1918

On the 21st of October, I was chosen in the first detachment to go to Naix to train for front-line trench work. We imitated working parties and learned to put up barbed wire. We became proficient in signaling, in the use of various implements, and in the use of gas masks under night conditions in dummy trenches some distance behind the line. In point of fact the trenches were twelve miles away. At least our initiation was conducted under shellfire. All night long there was a northeast gale blowing with rain and wind. We had no sleep and left early in the morning to return to Naix where we learned of the news that the *Antilles*[32] from our convoy had been sunk by a German submarine on the way back to America.

At Naix we had a well-remembered cabaret party, where a very good American singer from Mississippi sang, volunteering to sing all evening while we enjoyed the delectation of the wine. We had lots of drills here and practice in the use of gas masks, acquiring the standard proficiency in putting these on in six seconds. On the 30th we left for the trenches at Athienville and were convoyed there in big trucks sent from Paris for that purpose. I was left behind to take care of the baggage; however, I proceeded with it the next day and passed through Serres, which was two miles back of the third-line trenches. Here there were constant airplane battles going on, and I witnessed my first conflict of this kind. We saw them every day.

On the 2nd of November we left for the trenches one mile away and were, of course, in close range of the German guns all the time that we were at Athienville. The French were holding this position at this time. On

17

November 3rd I had my first experience in the trenches. During the night we relieved the French and took over the work. It was while this change was taking place that the Germans sent over their barrages according to custom and made a raid on our lines capturing and wounding many of us; hence, I was in the raid which occurred when the first American prisoners were taken in the war—twelve of them. They were in their dugouts. A force of several hundred Germans appeared at the door of the dugout and, holding hand grenades over their heads, said that they would blow all of the Americans to bits if a single man made a move. Of course, to save each other they had to surrender, as there were twelve men to several hundred Germans.[33]

The night of our first experience in the trenches lasted from 8:00 in the evening until 5:00 in the morning. It rained all night—so much so that the trenches had collapsed in many places. The mud was up to our knees. On the parapet[34] one man got stuck in the mud and sank further and further in while trying to pull first one foot out and then the other. I went over the parapet to try to get him out, but I was restrained by a machine gun. We finally got him out, but it took three of us to do it.

The bombing and shelling and rocketing going on here this night reminded me of a Fourth of July fireworks display at Manhattan Beach. At 5:00 a.m. we went back to our billets, much exhausted, cold and sore, and lay down to get some sleep to the tune of shells whizzing overhead. The Germans were getting the range of our dugout. The communications between the trenches were now in a demolished state. We had to work in the open a great deal. Things were comparatively quiet, however. We went out to the trenches every night for eight nights.

On the 4th of November we had our first working party. The French trench system required a new drainage system that we installed. Here, too, we were shelled for the first time. However, this was the quietest sector at the time along the whole battle front[35]—up to the date of our arrival. By a quiet sector it is not meant that the shelling ceased, but as for raids or real action, there was a mutual understanding between the French and Germans that if you do not fire at us, we will not fire at you. We changed all that. The Germans started a furious firing at the steeple of the church. Our guns way behind the lines began a furious cannonade of famous Strassburg,[36] the capital of Lorraine. A French officer who had not quite understood the changed condition of affairs had much difficulty in understanding that the French orders were now all changed, as we could not comply with his orders to not return the fire of the Germans. A court-martial was avoided when an American officer explained the new state of affairs. The French had claimed that it was a rest sector and wanted to keep it so. Our bombardment was the first shelling experienced at this place in many months.

In the early evening of November 4th, which was the night after the prisoners were taken by the Germans, our Captain made a speech to us and said, "Men, you have heard of the twelve prisoners taken last night from the 16th Infantry. I want to tell you that if any of your Company is taken prisoner, I shall expect the rest of you to go and get them back."

On November 9th we went to Serres and were shelled all along the route. On the 10th we went to Abainville where I got more letters from home. On the 12th we rested. I got word that the *Finland* was struck on her return trip and had turned back to St. Nazaire for repairs. On November 20th we went to Biencourt to complete the construction of cantonments. We also constructed stables for the artillery. On the 22nd we went to Bois de Gouverde and made more stables. We were here during the coldest days of that cold year. In the evening a detachment of artillery had come in from a hike and reported that one of their men had slipped with his horse on the ice and was killed. Here we learned of the famous British drive on Cambrai and that the Italians had checked the Germans on the Udine front.

At Athienville we went into training to repulse raids. Of actual raids the Germans only made one. In our house where we were quartered, the owner was arrested for being a spy. He was discovered with an underground telephone system, which led to the German trench. We then realized why it was that his house out of all the others in the town had never been touched by German shelling. We got plenty of wine in this town. [Ed. On November 23rd the First Division was issued General Order 67, which is included in the Appendix: 146.]

On November 26th I had my first supper of eggs and potatoes, which was a real relish in these days and much appreciated. I took a walk at night along a very dark and lonely road to Biencourt, four miles away. Here too I slept in my first French bed, and it felt like home compared to what I had been using. It had a mattress stuffed with feathers into which I sank a foot or more, and although there was no fire, we were given two hot bricks by the lady of the house. I experienced my first snowstorm in France. On November 28, 1917, Thanksgiving Day, some of us went to Abainville. Here there was a large celebration on the night of November 29th because turkey had arrived from the States. The following day we walked back to Demange, 20 miles away, all in one day. On this date I got my first letter from J.A.D.[37]

On December 1st we completed some stables we had been constructing. I spent my evenings here in a home with a large French dictionary. While I was here, we learned that the husband of the house had been taken prisoner and was in Germany. His wife, with whom some of us were sleeping, prepared innumerable boxes to send to him, but his letters showed that they were always pilfered of the food and tobacco before reaching him. They heard from each other quite regularly. The people of this town were very disconsolate about the war; they thought it would never end.

At this time the officer in charge of our outfit told us that since he was also a member of the intelligence department, he would be grateful to have us tell him of anything that looked suspicious or any suspicious news in the papers. He had seen an aspirin advertisement or a series of advertisements with the pills differing in number every few days, and he had learned it was notification of the departure and number of transports coming over. We were told to be careful of even the French people with whom we mingled, as many of them were reputed to be spies for Germany. Women, for instance, would signal airplanes by peculiar placing of their wash out on the lawns.[38]

On December 4th I road a horse for several miles along an icy road and fell twice without injury. At Biencourt I fell in with an interesting French family with daughters and was treated royally by the father with wine and real meals.

On December 7, 1917, America declared war on Austria-Hungary, and we believed that we would be sent to the Italian Front. On the 9th of December we went on a hike to a lumber camp and saw wild boars and German prisoners quartered within barbed wire. At Biencourt we were engaged mostly in constructing stables. On the 13th the famous Rainbow Division[39] passed through. One of their infantrymen stole our dictionary, but I got it back by going to his shack and taking it away from him. We had a report

Germans were approaching, and all the natives left the town. On the 15th all work was stopped.

By December 16th I completed reading *The Double Traitor*,[40] a book about France, Germany, and England before the war. On the 19th we went to Demange. We were at Demange for 21 days, from December 19, 1917, to January 9, 1918. On December 24th we had a banquet with twenty-four fellows including two lieutenants. The banquet will long be remembered. One of the lieutenants received word from General Pershing that the system got wind of forty-two spies in the division. We referred to them as "Double Traitors." On Christmas, I went to Mass. On the 28th of December, I got my first pass and went to Bar-le-Duc where I saw buildings that had been completely destroyed by bombs dropped from airplanes. I walked from Bar-le-Duc to Ligny. Here I was approached by a French infantryman who asked me how many Americans I thought were in France. He told me the French were tired of the war and wanted it over. [I evaded the question.] You see we had to be on our guard. On New Year's Eve we celebrated by going about town ringing Klaxon horns.[41]

On January 2, 1918, for the third time I put my name in for Officers' Training Corps. On the 4th we were given our first trench hats—that is, overseas caps. This day I met Kane of Georgetown, class of 1907. An American officer was caught throwing up signals to German aviators and was sent back to the States. On the 9th we returned to Abainville. Here for the first time we became acquainted with "Propergander"[42]—signs were all over. We trained in gas masks. On the 12th of January we had a hike of 12 kilometers,[43] and on the 13th of January we hiked for 12 more kilos. We had practice in hand grenade work and liquid fire drills.

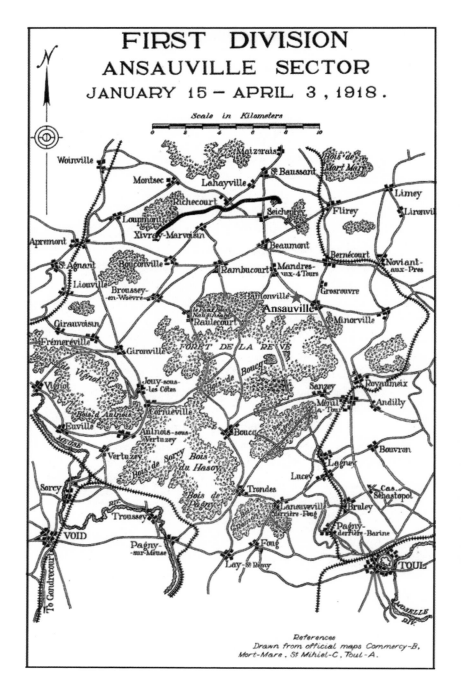

Figure 9: Map of Ansauville Sector[44]

IV

TOUL-ANSAUVILLE SECTOR

JANUARY 15 – APRIL 6, 1918

During the next two and one-half months we sojourned at Mauvages, Sorcy, Jouy-sous-les-Côtes (Joy Among the Hills), Camp de Gerard SAS, Rambucourt (Montsec), Raulecourt, Camp Essayons,[45] Amarillo, Sanzey, and Maron. This period culminated and finished our military training, which resulted in our being fully-trained soldiers ready for any action.

On January 15, 1918, the Division received orders to be on the move. The enlisted man very seldom has information of the destination but gets prepared to march along until the command comes to halt. We all knew by the preparations that it was farewell to Abainville.

After a march of twelve miles we halted for the night at a town called Mauvages. The heavy fall of snow rendered the journey a mighty disagreeable one, and our wet, sore feet added to our discomfort. We dried out thoroughly by the fireplaces in the French houses and were soon ready for bed and the hayloft. At five o'clock the next morning we were on the move again, coming on the 17th to Sorcy. The snow had turned to heavy rain. We visited many private houses where we were entertained royally. Since the law compelled all wine shops to close at 7 p.m., hospitality in private homes was greatly appreciated. On the 18th we went to Jouy-sous-les-Côtes, arriving at six o'clock in the evening. Pretty well-fatigued after this thirty-mile hike, I forfeited my supper to get rest. The burden of a full pack and poor roads had made the long journey more tedious.

We did a lot of hiking at this time and slept in haylofts mostly. I was now Acting Sergeant. While here we had training in trench warfare and drilling in demolition work. On the 20th at Jouy we entered a house which had

23

been vacated. Inside we found all the furniture sealed up. Upon breaking open a bureau, we found it contained some excellent table silver and some very valuable mathematical instruments. When some of our men were about to take these away with them, an officer entered and ordered us to put them back, which we of course did, and then we left. Later, when we went back to the house, we found the mathematical instruments gone, and of course concluded that the officer had taken them.

The three days spent here in Jouy-sous-les-Côtes were devoted to demolition and instructions in the French method of putting up barbed wire. However, ample leisure was had, which enabled me to visit Fort Jouy situated on a high hill that overlooked the vast area held by the Germans. The outline of the German trenches could be distinctly discerned while the impregnable Montsec proudly towered above the surrounding hills. These hills were prominently located in the center of our sector which we later took over from the French. Here an unobstructed view was had of these indomitable positions which were well-fortified with artillery of every description. Little did I suspect at this time that my Division eight months later would batter their way through these fortifications in a famous attack capturing Montsec and the village of St. Mihiel, for I knew the attempt had been made by the French who could only retreat with the loss of thirty thousand men. And little did I imagine that my Division would attempt to break down these German strongholds, which for four years had been strengthened and made secure from any attack.

For one hour I stood on the parapet of this huge fort entranced by this wonderful panorama comprising the sector we were about to take over. Not a suspicion of the tragedy to follow clouded the pleasure of the moment; the beauty of the surrounding country and clear view of the whole tableau seemed to hold me fast. This was my first idea of any war theatre and the first picture of the battle front. I could readily understand how a comparatively few men could ward off attack by superior numbers. I retraced my steps toward camp and learned of orders to move.

On the 21st we were on the march again. We arrived at Camp de Gerard SAS, seven miles behind the front line trenches, where we were billeted[46] in barracks. There were many airplanes flying about taking photographs. Here we found that the First Division of the American Army had received the honor of taking over the Toul Sector from the French. It had been a quiet sector under the French, but we changed all that.

On the 22nd the Germans opened up a barrage preparatory for a raid. They thought presumably to take us unaware, such as to what had occurred in the Sommerviller Sector. This time every man was ready. When the attack reached the middle of no-man's-land,[47] our artillery made a counterbarrage. We met the Hun[48] with machine gun and rifle bullets, thus forcing the Germans to retreat, leaving many dead and wounded, while the First Division gloried in its achievement on repelling a raid for the first time. Some Germans, finding that they were caught in a trap, threw down their arms and raised their hands shouting, "*Kamerad, Kamerad.*"[49] This trick did not work, and we burned out fifteen machine guns on this occasion, killing four hundred of them.[50] There was a distance of thirty yards between the trenches.

Four of us continued the next day to a town called Raulecourt, five kilos from the front line, for schooling on road building. This town was void of inhabitants and from appearances must have received its share of shelling during the onslaught at the beginning of the war. No house was wholly intact. Where I was billeted, my bed was set close up against an outset in the wall which had been pierced by a shell, cutting a hole five feet wide. A French sergeant under whom we were receiving instructions informed me that I had the bed in which he slept at the time this shell struck.

We hiked twelve miles to repair roads and visited the artillery emplacements of the French. As part of our training we repaired trenches and wire entanglements. We fortified the reserve trenches and worked on the roads three miles behind the lines. During this time we also constructed and repaired dugouts and made them gas-proof. By now we began to believe there would be no end to the war. Here we saw the sun for the first time since we arrived in France. All night we could hear the bombing of guns in the distance, and all day we could hear the shell firing that was going on to destroy communications, ammunition dumps, roads, and railroads.

On the 24th we surveyed roads. We could plainly see the German encampments on the hills in the distance, and they, too, had a clear observation of our areas from their hills. The next day we worked on the roads again, all the while [German] airplanes were hovering overhead in conflict with our anti-aircraft guns. One night while I was asleep, a German shell blew out the side of the room in which I slept.

The Germans often used deceptive techniques. During patrol work the Germans would come over and purportedly surrender to our sentries. We were advised when taking prisoners who yelled "*Kamerad*" to be on our

Living History

RELIEF OF ANSAUVILLE SECTOR[51]

Operations Section, General Staff
Field Orders

1st Division, A.E.F.,
Gondrecourt, Meuse,
January 14, 1918.

No. 1

[Extract]

1. In conformance with the instructions of the French First Army, the Moroccan Division and the French 69th Division, the troops of this division enumerated below will relieve the corresponding units of the Moroccan Division in the Ansauville subsector.

> 1st Brigade
> **1st Engr. Regiment (less 1st Bn.)**
> **Engineer train**
> Detachment 2d Field Bn. Signal Corps
> Headquarters Troop
> Co. No. 1, Military Police
> Det. Ambulance Co. No. 2 (horse)
> Det. Ambulance Co. No. 13 (motor)

******

By command of Major General Bullard:
Campbell King,
Chief of Staff.

United States Army Center of Military History (1998), "Training and Use of American Units with the British and French," *United States Army in World War I*, version 2, CD-ROM disc 1 of 3, volume III: 464.

guard, compel them to kneel with their hands up, and advance on them with loaded gun ready for [German] treachery. On other occasions we learned Germans had been spying in Allied[52] uniforms, or in snow time they would wear white garments.

When we went into the trenches for the first time, we could distinctly hear the German band playing in the opposite trench not 100 yards from us. In fact, we used to call the Germans over when they displayed a desire to hear our phonograph that we had in the trench. When we got them over, we took them prisoners. About 200 of them, including officers, really gave themselves up.[53] [Embellishing stories while working in the trenches was common.]

Preparations were underway for the training in repelling raids and making raids. Elaborate systems were designed along a more substantial line. The roads all the way to the [front] lines were camouflaged then repaired. Trenches were strengthened, and dugouts both at the lines and in the neighboring towns were quickly constructed and reinforced. The work of running the barbed wire was entrusted to me, so with my detail each night I was obliged to traverse over torn up roads and fields and through a badly battered town.

On one occasion when nearing our place of work, the Germans began the evening with a gas attack. Donning our masks we attempted to move about and continue on. As it was a black night and rather difficult to see out of our masks, a few of us fell into trenches or in shell holes, and some even were headed in the wrong direction. It took us a good part of the night to find our way, and, hence, there was practically no work done. I remember being called up for this, and I was hard pressed to convince anyone that we resorted to the gas mask, as they had no report of such an attack in camp. Later reports from the lines verified this incident, and it was considered a severe attack.

At another time we were digging a drain which extended well out into no-man's-land. Evidently we were observed, for the Germans drove us undercover with an impromptu barrage. Things here were a little more lively, and I could not see how this sector was considered a quiet one. However, I was always ready to leave when the next detail arrived; there was no delay either, for invariably the Germans shelled our area. One night especially a general bombardment was on just as we left the trenches. The sickening sirens of these shells as they passed overhead and the deadly explosion that followed traveled with us. During the trip to camp I counted forty-five shells fired at an artillery dump in the woods two hundred yards from me. Of these, twenty-five shells were duds while the rest exploded with no damage until the forty-fifth, when the whole heavens were lit up by the mass of artillery shells exploding. The Germans had made a hit, but at a considerable expense.

All through the next day the excitement continued. The clear sky overhead gave opportunity for many air battles. At one time a German plane could be seen coming out of a cloud when an Allied plane would give chase. The machine gun fire could be distinctly heard as the two planes attacked each other, jockeying here and there until the German plane was driven to its lines. Often a German aviator was about reconnoitering[54] when suddenly a barrage of shrapnel[55] would halt him on his expedition. The anti-aircraft guns about the vicinity would blaze away with shells bursting in the air seeming as though each one was a hit, only to find the German plane flying away towards home apparently unharmed.

Continual shell firing was kept up for three days both by our artillery and the German artillery, each endeavoring to blow up fortifications, dumps, or strong points. Frequently gas masks were worn throughout the night; when the alarm would sound, we all would don the mask and often fall asleep with it on.

By this time everyone knew of the strongly fortified position of the Germans and their one dreadful observation post on Montsec from where an unobstructed view of our whole area could be had. On February 2, 1918, commencing at eight o'clock in the evening, our heavy artillery bombarded Montsec for one hour. From our town a good view of this cannonading[56] could be had, so we all congregated on a camouflaged road and watched these big six-inch shells tear their way through the peak of this hill. Although it was dark and Montsec was five miles away, we could see when a bull's eye was made by the ball of fire belching forth as the shells exploded. Despite this terrific attack, the next morning Montsec seemed undisturbed; but we knew the Germans realized we were ready for them. From now on it was give and take, and there was no cessation to this duel. German aeroplane[57] activity made an unusual demonstration about our area, bombing emplacements and our front lines.

We were now drawn from our work at the lines and ordered to Essayons where we broke ground for cantonments. Here we lived while we repaired the roads leading to the lines, for they were impassable; and artillery could not be hastened forward. With only three miles between the German lines and us, repairing roads was not a very pleasant task; the shelling and aeroplane bombardment kept us seeking cover continually. I knew something exciting was about to take place, and did materialize, when on the 23rd of February we were ordered to the lines, arriving there at six o'clock in the evening. The infantry was to make its first raid on the enemy.

We entered the lines during the rage of a terrific snowstorm where a hurricane gale blew the icy flakes in a blinding fashion through the trenches. It was not till the orders came to load and fix bayonets that a thrill set our blood tingling and relieved our chilly bones. As the hour approached for the opening of hostilities, when the artillery would blaze a trail ahead for the doughboys,[58] excitement ran rampant. It was now 7:45 and all eyes centered on the front lines eagerly awaiting the red flares that signaled the artillery in the rear. At eight o'clock the stillness would be broken and overcome by a din of shot and shell unparalleled by anything of its kind here since the beginning of the war. All of a sudden the artillery let fly a shower of lead that shook the very earth, and the doughboys in orderly fashion followed the barrage closely. Machine guns from the right and left flank kept up an incessant fire, sweeping no-man's-land, and driving any enemy patrol to shelter. Montsec for the second time during our sojourn here was unmercifully bombarded while the sky about us was illuminated by the vast balls of fire bursting from its peak. A multitude of shells coming from the rear sent their deadly siren echoing for miles as they sped on for destruction.

The German lines were entered, and much to our surprise only a few prisoners were taken, and these were left there to protect the retreat of the others. With the protection of the barrage, the infantry returned rejoicing in their success—their first raid, first to enter the enemy's lines, and first to take prisoners. Gradually calm and quietude prevailed, and orders came to be ready and alert. All expected a counterattack by the Germans, but still we waited, and still the heavy onslaught of snow swept through our trenches. Not a sound was heard for the rest of the night, but just before daybreak orders came to again be ready. This is usually the hour for a raid or an attack. Much to our relief at nine o'clock we marched from the lines to our camp at Essayons for food and sleep.

On March 1, 1918, we drew nearer to the lines, making our home at Amarillo, which place we later gave the name of Shrapnel Hollow. Here we were located in a hollow fifty feet wide between two battered and shell-torn hills. There was a small French detachment in the vicinity, and at this point the French lines joined ours. In the hill facing the lines, the French had constructed dugouts thirteen feet underground. These dugouts contained bunks for twenty men—ten upper and ten lower berths. The upper berths were not so bad, but the lower berths would very often be submerged in water. The few pumps we had were continually operating; yet, although the dugouts would be well pumped out, during the night the water would seep through and all but cover the bottom berths, necessitating a few contortive moments for those sleeping there to extricate themselves.

On the other hill was located a battery of artillery, also well known to the enemy. Barrage after barrage would take place while for hours a steady gas attack would be launched, endeavoring to drive our artillery out. Thirty men on one occasion were blinded by this gas attack, as they had removed their masks from their face in order to get range. Night after night we would be awakened by the guard warning us of gas. The Klaxon horns at the front lines would give the signal, and this would be taken up all through the area as far back as Raulecourt seven miles away. I often sat at the entrance to my dugout and watched the shells tearing up the hill and uprooting trees in their effort to destroy the artillery. Big clogs of dirt and mud would be hurled at you if you did not hasten to shelter.

In the evening of the 3rd of March we were ordered to the lines. At seven o'clock the Germans opened up a vicious barrage with tear gas and mustard gas.[59] Assembling in the Hollow was a vast amount of human beings and mules, as the rations had just been brought up. Shells were breaking about while a dud struck but two feet from me. The mules weathered the attack undisturbed. With the barrage still raging and seeming as though getting heavier and heavier every minute, we double-quick timed[60] it towards the trenches. With gas masks on, it was extremely difficult to make rapid progress, and unfortunately we lost direction of our position. A private just returning from the lines and who was familiar with the lay of the land led the way as a guide. He brought orders that the Germans were on their way over and to make haste. Falling into shell holes, tripping over barbed wire, and in almost an exhausted state, we finally reached our place and readied for action. The soldiers of the 18th American Regiment who were occupying the front lines were holding fast, but the Hun got over, killing many and taking a few prisoners. Orders soon came for our relief, and for the rest of the night there were peace and tranquility. The next morning the camp was busy making crosses for the graves of the dead doughboys.

Things were exceptionally quiet this day, and as I had charge of the pumping squad, I managed to get the opportunity to visit the French sector. Walking through the Hollow, I first came across a huge concrete foundation supporting one of the French naval guns. This gun had not been used for some time, as its range was too long for this sector. Located on the hill opposite was a cleverly constructed dummy gun, which consisted of a log painted black protruding from a foundation and carefully camouflaged. The barrel of the gun was the only part seen. To an unsuspecting observer the dummy gun appeared as the genuine thing, and from the battering the emplacement received with shell holes everywhere and trees that at one time protected it now torn up, I judged the Germans also were deceived. Thousands of dollars were no doubt spent in storming this supposed strongpoint, which contained nothing but a log. I continued on down the Hollow for quite a ways and found nothing more to interest me as everything was torn up by shells. I then went out on the road and crossed to the thick forest in which the French had their numerous canteens.

Keeping to the edge of this forest and just inside, so as not to be observed, I walked on to the end where the third-line trench was and which gave me an excellent view of the whole battle area. Our sector extended for five miles. Beginning at this dense forest where I stood, the trench system was laid out in zigzag fashion where on our extreme left we joined the French. Extending out for two hundred yards lay no-man's-land, a complete mass of shell holes which gave evidence of many attacks and counterattacks. Beyond this area were the German barbed wire entanglements, which were in front of their first, second, and third-line trenches. Just in the rear of the third-line [trenches] and on our left center towered this rock of Gibraltar—Montsec.

Although the artillery emplacements were not visible, I could picture their positions, for every place of vantage could be conjectured. In the center and extending for miles was open level country, and in the distance

Living History

ASSEMBLY OF UNITS 1ST DIVISION UPON RELIEF[61]

3d Bureau, General Staff
No. 1562/3

French Eighth Army,
April 1, 1918.

SPECIAL ORDER NO. 349

I. The elements of the American 1st Division now stationed in the zone of the XXXII Army Corps will be assembled as follows after their relief by the American 26th Division:

Hq.: GONDREVILLE

Infantry: Hq. 2d Brigade, 26th and 28th Regts. Signal Battalion, Divisional Machine Gun Battalion, Brigade Machine Gun Battalion, in the zone: GONDREVILLE–VELAINE-en-HAYE–Poste de VELAINE–Camp Bois de l'EVEQUE–PIERRE-la-TREICHE–GONDREVILLE, all these localities inclusive.

Artillery: In the zone: LAGNEY–BOUVRON–ECROUVES–GRANDMENIL–LANEUVEVILLE-derriere-FOUG–LAGNEY, all these localities inclusive

Engineers and Engineer train: MARON and SEXEY-aux-FORGES.

Trains: Commander of trains and detachment of police ambulance and sanitary trains, ammunition trains, E. M. R., supply train, at TOUL.

The billeting facilities of the cantonment reserve for the 1st Div. has been communicated to the staff of the 1st Division.

******

PASSAGA.

United States Army Center of Military History (1998), "Training and Use of American Units with the British and French," *United States Army in World War I*, version 2, CD-ROM disc 1 of 3, volume III: 487.

could be seen the hills and forests bordering on Alsace. Once a prosperous farming district, it was now a torn up and battered waste land. Scattered about through this area could be seen the French villages apparently untouched. The church steeple was plainly observed and evidently afforded a lookout station for the German scouts. I thought now that no doubt this area would always be German until the end of the war, since for four years the Germans held these positions, and no attempt had been made to arrest these positions from the Germans since the disaster to the French.

I retraced my steps to camp with no notice given to the shelling going on. I emerged from the woods and walked the tracks of a narrow gauge railroad, which the French had laid. Just then a shrieking shell came over, and I ducked when it struck one of the rails; it exploded throwing and killing a Frenchman who was walking twenty-five yards in front of me. I did not know what else might be coming, so I lost no time in getting to my dugout, helping the Frenchmen carry their comrade down into the Hollow.

For one whole week now—morning, afternoon, and night—the Germans would send over one barrage after another, and in turn the Americans would counterattack with a barrage. The area was saturated with gas. Fellows using towels had their faces all inflamed, some with their skin turned brown, and others with eyes swollen. Men walked around gasping for breath and coughing violently. Orders were given now to keep gas masks on; the gas masks were not to be removed till we were ordered to do so. Meals were delayed while the uncovered food had to be destroyed. By this time we were getting mighty sick of living here continually wearing a gas mask, continually being driven into our dugouts, continually hurrying to the lines, and no sleep. This sector we thought was a quiet sector, so we asked each other, "What must it be like at a lively sector?"

On the 12th of March the French staged a raid. They called upon the American artillery to assist in the barrage, which they did. The combined French and American artillery was too much for the Germans. The French went over bringing back 100 prisoners.

On the 15th of March, I was in charge of a detail on constructing shelters just back of the third-line trenches. A squad of infantry was sent over to assist, and I noted one of the fellows was under guard. I got talking to this fellow and asked why he was under arrest. He said it was for being A.W.O.L.[62] He told me that last night he wanted to go over to no-man's-land

and explore. Crawling out underneath our wire on his stomach, he crossed no-man's-land. When the German patrol came along, he lay quietly till they passed. Going a little further and in the light of the flares going up, he came across a form on the ground. Not knowing if he was dead, he drew his pistol and watched. As he saw no movement, he advanced and waited for another flare. This cold light shining on the man's features showed he was a corpse. The prisoner turned to me and said, "Say, Buddy, don't you think I wasn't scared either. I wanted souvenirs, so going through the fellow's pockets, I got these photographs." He showed me about five pictures of German soldiers and other pictures taken in Germany.

Well this squad of infantry was not much for working. They said they did not mind fighting, but when it came to pick and shovel, they were not putting out, as it was called. When they learned that we had to work and fight, too, it was no incentive for them to transfer to the engineers. Fortunately we were not bombarded during this work, so in three days we had three of these shelters completed. It was an unusual quietude that prevailed for the last few days, and I thought it was just a calm before a storm.

We learned of a report that a number of spies had recently been captured in the lines. One was found with the number and location of our guns and also the time we fired our guns. Another was caught in front of my dugout. He was dressed in an American uniform with a French helmet on and no gas mask. He was sent to headquarters for not having credentials.

Orders came on the 30th of March to break camp. Contrary to expectations the usual bombardment did not occur as relief took place. However, we did not feel safe until we reached Camp Essayons. From here we hiked to Sanzey. This was quite a town whose reputation was known by the number of cafés here. On the 1st of April after a journey of eighteen miles, we arrived at Maron, a town of goodly size and more to the liking of us Americans. Here we were to remain for two weeks, mainly attending lectures and undergoing drills.

On Wednesday, April 3rd,[63] came an opportunity for me to learn a bit about the banking system of France. About three kilometers from Maron is located the town of Neuves-Maisons, and it is our custom when stationed in a village for a few days to ascertain the whereabouts of the largest town near us. Well Neuves-Maisons was my objective. For months I had been endeavoring to cash a check, or rather a draft on a bank in Paris, and, after visiting towns where this bank had its representatives, was informed that Paris was the only place to go. At this time it was impossible for me to make the trip. After an exchange of letters between the banking house and me, a solution was found by means of a money order. It was to Neuves-Maisons I went to see about this.

To facilitate matters I needed to take along one who could speak French. As there were quite a few men in my Company who professed to be an expert in this, I soon found one, Private R. I had more reasons than one for asking this fellow, one of which was that there never seemed to be much trouble in his getting wine, whether we had money or not. As the best transportation to be had was our feet, we set out. At first I was rather uneasy because stringent orders were given me, and I was absolutely responsible for the conduct and safe return of Private R. This fellow was a keen observer, and before we hardly got started, one of the thousand cafés in France was situated directly in our path. There was nothing else to do but become acquainted with our French neighbor. No doubt if the location was not surrounded with the beauty of France, we would have made our journey in record time.

As it was, we lingered, and handicapped as I was in not knowing the language, the attention of the barmaid was well taken care of by my friend while I enjoyed the luscious *hic, haec, hoc* (wine).[64] While with assurance we would call again, we said "Good-bye" and continued our journey. We walked along the edge of a canal with the hilly woods on our right and the quiet restful waters of the canal on our left, while the left bank of the canal was beautified by the dark green fields and the graveled roads winding through them—scenery for which all France is noted. Soon we reached the concrete bridge, spanning the canal by fifty or sixty feet, with artistic iron railings along its sides. Approaching our town, we found a few minutes to chat with the Algerians[65] who were quartered here and who informed us that most anything one would wish could be purchased here. This information was news, as it was the first time that anyone expressed belief that clothes could be bought anywhere outside of Paris, and it was my wonder what the peasants wore.

After learning the whereabouts of the post office, we proceeded there. There was first a formal introduction between Private R. and the French Postmaster. After telling Private R. what I wanted, I then sat down. It took

fifteen minutes of the worst struggle with the French language, shaking of
fingers, and waving of hands before I came to realize that the check was
not to be cashed by a money order and that our fight was with the Boche[66]
and not the French. I gave it up and had Paris return the money to the
States. I guess it was pretty well hacked up after going through so many
hands. I learned from this that only the city and bank to which the draft,
check, money order, or such is made out can cash it. It was so in this case,
anyway, but I thank France that she was selling wine at this time.

We soon forgot the incident and tried other means of making news. We
found the means. When it was time to return, my troubles began, as my last
instructions given before leaving camp appeared written in the big expanse
of the horizon. A short walk brought us to the bridge crossing the canal,
with the stone wall that approached the entrance to the bridge possessing
a wonderful attraction for the weary. Straddling this wall was Private R.
with no intention of getting home. Persuasion prevailed and after a half-
hour, on we trod. A short distance, however, was long enough, for again
the soft bank of the canal was enticing, and again did Private R. embarrass
my plans for a speedy return. This time persuasion was not so powerful, so
I left trusting that the good gods would arouse the stupid fool. They soon
did, and while I was quite a distance ahead, Private R. soon caught up; and
we were now but a few steps from our camp.

Alas and alack, an especially good friend came along and, darn, if he
did not take Private R. back with him to Neuves-Maisons. Disgust was but
a small portion of my feelings going into camp alone. As Private R. slept in
the same billet as I, he woke me up at eleven o'clock that night, having been
brought in by a sergeant from another village. It happened that Private R.,
thinking he was in the right town and accustomed to climbing up a ladder
to his bunk, did so in this village which happened to be the billet where the
sergeant slept. He was recognized and escorted back home and thanks to
something, someone, or somebody, Private R.'s absence was not known. I
do not care to dwell upon court-martials. The incident was a secret for I am
still sergeant.

At this time there was a great deal of excitement over the Cambrai drive
where the English were crowning themselves with glory. Report had it that
the Germans were being driven in the attack by [their own] machine guns,

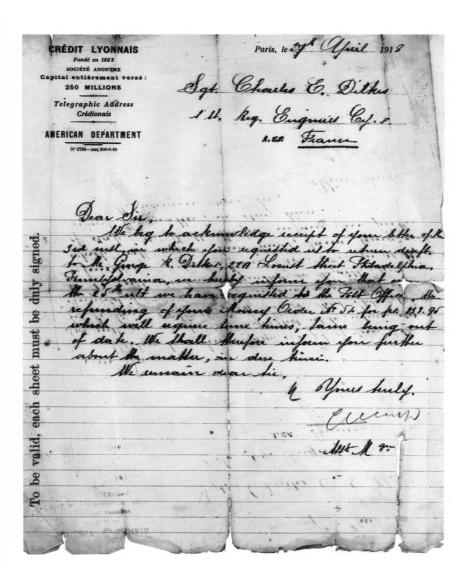

Figure 10: Letter from Crédit Lyonnais Bank

and it was either advance or be killed by their own machine gunmen. The report continued to state that the English were administering a terrific loss to the Germans and the fighting was stubborn on both sides. Amidst all this news we were called out for drill with full equipment, the significance of which we were to learn later.

The next morning was devoted to more drills. In the afternoon the whole village of Maron turned out, as though it was a holiday, for the excitement of a football game. The town people were enthusiastic football fans who came to watch a game between the 1st and 2nd Battalions, which resulted in a defeat for my battalion. Later it was officially announced that the Germans made a treacherous attack on the division which relieved us in the trenches at the Toul Sector and, in addition to taking the trenches, drove the [Allied] troops back a mile and took possession of a town called Mandres. The trenches were soon retaken with a considerable loss of life. It is here I may state that at no time, so far, did the First Division lose any portion of the trenches held by them. Moreover, I can go further by stating that in every raid the Germans made on the First Division, the First Division held the lines at the Toul Sector, and the Germans not once reached our front line. [Ed. Charles Edward Dilkes noted General Orders 119, 123, and 16 and tributes from Major General Bullard and General Marchand, which are included in the Appendix: 147+.]

Well a new form of amusement was held in the evening which consisted of throwing sous[67] to the Algerian soldiers to watch them fight for them. Their enthusiasm soon got the best of them and fights ensued while the sous lay where they fell. The kids in the village, being spectators, took advantage of this temporary cessation of gold hunting by the Algerians and fought for the sous themselves. This soon angered the Algerian soldiers, and only the interference of the Americans avoided a clash between the native villagers and the Algerians.

On April 6th the regiment was assembled before the Major who informed us that tomorrow we leave to go into actual combat. To put it as it was stated, he said, "Men, we will now cease to be tin soldiers. We are going after the Boche, and it will not be a quiet sector." He went on to say that all of us would not come out of this sector alive, and that this sector was considered one of the main points of attack by the Germans. He depicted the whole thing as being a general slaughter. He outlined the work required for the engineers, and after he finished, no one thought his life was worth a penny. His depiction was to us as it was read: our whole regiment, no doubt, would be wiped out before we got through with our operations, and, in a few words, every shell coming over had a name on it—one for each individual in the regiment. We ourselves could not conceive of any worst place than the sector we had just left, the Toul Sector. Although there was no one killed from my Company while we served in the Toul Sector, it was lively enough. I could not say the outlook for where we were going was pleasant, but a little more action was what we wanted.

We left the next morning, April 7th, at six o'clock for Neufmaisons where we embarked on trains, becoming familiar with "*40 hommes—8 chevaux.*" No one seemed to know our destination, but we all knew the French people hated to see us leave Maron where many francs, of course, were left. That night we spent a miserable time in the famous side door Pullman cars with but little sleep. The morning found us riding through the towns of Vallentigny, Troyes, and Chalmaison—all large cities boasting of their palatial dwellings, hotels, restaurants, etc. We also passed through St. Julien, and at 6:30 p.m. we passed around the outskirts of Paris and cities such as Nogent, Perreux-Sur-Marne, Noisy-le-Sec, and others.

Tuesday, April 9th, found us at a town called Persan where we all unloaded, and details were sent out to help the artillery unload their cannons, mules, and wagons. Having arrived at Persan at one o'clock in the morning, this unloading kept the companies standing around till all were ready to move on, which brought the time up to four o'clock. We then proceeded in search of billets. At 4:30 we found these billets in a large manufacturing plant. The appearance of the rooms resembled the ground floor of a huge office building. Here fatigued as we were, it was everyone for himself. There was no time lost in unslinging equipment, and all were soon glorying in sound slumber, completely done in with the long train ride and loss of sleep.

Our peaceful repose was of short duration, for at 6:30 an urgent call came for all hands to be up and to prepare for immediate departure. At 8:30 we were on the move again—hiking, hiking, hiking—when at five o'clock in the afternoon, after covering twenty miles, we arrived at a town but a couple of kilometers from Paris, Beaumont-le-Sec. We were completely exhausted from such a hike with practically no sleep for two days. On the command to halt and fall out, we did fall out, eager to get our blistered and aching feet off the ground and packs from our backs. Again we were distributed among billets and, for the first time, enjoyed undisturbed slumber.

The next morning we were aroused at five o'clock, ate breakfast, and continued the journey, leaving at 7:00 a.m.—another twenty miles and another bunch of sore, disgusted, and tired men. It was too much for some, so one by one they were forced to find rest by the roadside. These were left to the mercy of the hospital wagons, while for me the journey was halted in time; otherwise, I would soon be forced to join the rest of the sinking crew. I can tell you I had about enough, so you can all imagine our joy when a rest was declared for the next day. At this time we found the most rest in the cafés where *vin rouge*[68] helped us forget the trials and hardships of the past few days. On April 12th we found ourselves going through the usual routine of drill with lectures and reports on the progress of the war. We gladly listened to these reports which predicted the steady downfall of the Germans at the Somme, but we discouragingly finished up with word that we hike again in the morning.

However, instead of hiking I found myself Corporal of the Guard[69] and, hence, could not participate in the vaudeville performance at night given by members of the regiment. At 12:00 the pleasant evening turned to be one of the most miserable in France. A driving rain, a cold and blowing gale, was anything but pleasant for one doing guard duty all night. The next afternoon, however, we found time to entrench ourselves in billets and to forget everything in an eight-hour slumber. Awakened, however, by the timely bugler calling all for retreat, I got up but was excused from this formation.

To pass away the few minutes before supper, I repaired to the corral. There you find the mule skinners all busy grooming the animals before sundown.[70] One Italian, an interesting young chap who is a minister in civil life, was busy refuting arguments against the Italian soldier as a fighter. On this question he was being joshed considerably, but on my appearance found relief when I asked him to tell me about it. His father was at present conspicuous in the Italian Army as a general. I thought there was interesting news to be found.

The reign of Teutonic accretions, as you know, invaded Russia with the result that Russia was tottering, relieving the Germans of a great burden on the Eastern Front, and which allowed the Germans to give their attention to

Italy. Through intrigue, deceit, and connivance they soon prevailed upon the Commanding General of the Italian forces to enter into an alliance with France, Russia, and Germany whereby Italy would sell out to Germany. France would do the same, and this combination would attack England. This Italian general, unbeknown to his superiors, sold out for millions, and as planned, the Austrian soldiers were allowed to advance 30 miles in automobiles, taking 285,000 Italian soldiers as prisoners. They were only resisted by non-commissioned officers of the Italian Army.

After the Austrians had taken the large city of Udine, France nipped their plot before it materialized, while both the generals were convicted and have since paid the penalty. Here I readily imagined why Germany still entertained hopes of becoming victorious. Germany's success with Russia and this Austrian operation, if it had been consummated, would result in the whole of Germany exerting all its strength on her Western foes, as America had not as yet entered the lines for attack. Germany was well on her way to being conqueror. You, too, can understand that it was America that saved the day.

While Germany was enjoying all these successes, on Wednesday, April 17th, we renewed our strenuous hike to the front. We walked fifteen miles arriving at Jouy-le-Grand at 2:00 in the afternoon. Here we rested for the night, but we were called for assembly at 3:30 a.m. the next morning when for some reason or other the orders were changed—only to go into effect the same day. So on April 18th we left Jouy-le-Grand at 5:00 in the morning, hiked twenty miles to Pagny, then six more to Bonlier. Here we now commenced to hear the artillery sending its salute to Germany. We began to get interested when we reached Noyers-Saint-Martin, a town frequently visited by Boche planes. An interesting spectacle also was the heavy snowstorm lasting through a great part of the morning. This was little expected at this time, but nothing surprised us in France.

On April 21st we found ourselves resting quietly in Noyers-Saint-Martin. In the evening we enjoyed a lecture by an artillery major who stated his reason for entering the service, saying that it is known through all military channels that Germany's intentions are to exact a large indemnity from the United States; and rather than have this extortion happen, he is here to give his best to combat such notions. His speech was being accompanied by the heavy guns sending their mighty welcome to the Boche. All the next day was a continual roar of guns with a short intermission at night. Where we were going we were told there was no covering of any kind to shield us from shells. It promised to be an interesting spot no doubt, for we could not conceive of any place along the lines without its trench or dugout. On April 25th the Division was on the move once more. After an hour's march the whole Division, with various units coming in from all directions, converged at this point. This was an indication that our wearisome journey was at an end.

After a delay of three hours, our regiment disentangled itself from this mass of troops and, after marching for three miles, came to the town of Varmaise,[71] about eight miles from the front line trenches. Here we were quartered while neighboring towns billeted the other units of the Division. Because artillery action was quiet, we were not exactly certain of our location and did not think the lines were very close by. Soon, however, things began to slowly happen. The town of Varmaise had but few inhabitants; most of them left but a short time ago when the Germans were halted at the neighboring town of Montdidier in their attack on Paris. Twenty-five persons comprised the population of this town now, whereas the accommodations indicated a thriving little village of three or four hundred before the Germans intruded. Few houses had been bombed, but the fields were considerably torn up. There was no incentive for the peasants to proceed with farming, and it was only out of anxiety for their property that the few who were here remained. We were soon made as comfortable as could be expected, sleeping by sections in the lofts of the barns.

Living History

ANSAUVILLE SECTOR[72]

The First Division relieved the First Moroccan Division on January 15th, 1918, in the Ansauville Sector, north of Toul. This sector covered a front of seven and a half kilometers.

A raid was made by the enemy against the Third Battalion of the 18th Infantry on March 1st, 1918. On March 11th the Division made two raids against the enemy.

The Division was relieved between April 3rd and 5th, 1918 by the 26th American Division.

During its tour in the Ansauville Sector the Division captured ten prisoners.

1st casualties amounted to:

> Killed – 6 officers, 103 men;
> Wounded – 31 officers, 398 men;
> Missing – 1 officer, 3 men;
> Total – 38 officers, 504 men.

Commendations of First Division American Expeditionary Forces 1917 – 1919 France * Germany: 15

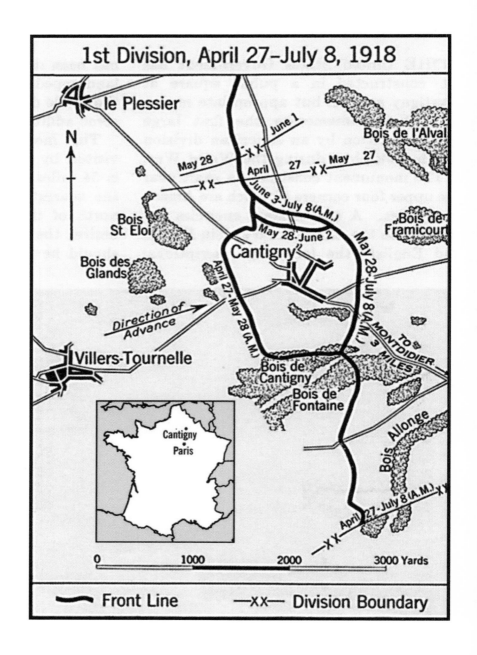

Figure 11: Map of Battle for Cantigny[73]

V

THE STORMING OF CANTIGNY

CANTIGNY SECTOR (OISE)

The infantry took over the front lines, relieving the French. The artillery immediately got their guns in place, ready at a moment's call, and allowed part of the French artillery to withdraw their guns. However, the heavy artillery of the French remained with us for support, with guns located about four miles from the lines, but firing into Montdidier ten miles away. The French artillery was utilized mostly for bombarding German fortifications in conjunction with our Division's heavy artillery, while our light artillery wholly replaced the French light artillery. The settlement was complete now for what later proved to be one of the biggest factors in prosecuting the War to a successful conclusion: the storming of Cantigny. The strategy was to have well-planned operations leading up to the attack, and to plan the final entry of the 1st Division infantry and engineers into the town.

At last the 1st Division became the first American forces to enter the lines as a real active fighting Division. With Chepoix as the engineers' headquarters, we commenced our operations preliminary to the storming of Cantigny. Chepoix was a town of good size, two kilometers from our station at Varmaise towards the German front lines, and within artillery fire from the German guns.

Cantigny, the town held by the Germans, was nothing but a mass of ruins situated on a towering hill with neighboring hills at the outskirts. On these hills the Germans had observation of the whole surrounding country, easily seeing our troops and trains of ammunition vehicles coming along the roads. All roads were held in danger by the German artillery guns; all paths marking the route of troops to and from our front lines were in line of fire from both the German machine guns and their artillery guns. German sharpshooters, snipers, and outposts had little trouble observing all our movements. This scrutiny, coupled with the observations taken by the enemies' airplanes, rendered our work and positions the most dangerous along the whole front. This vantage post that the enemy controlled prompted us to develop a strategy to take the heights while at the same time uplift the morale of our Allies.

Everything depended on our success here. It was as if all the Allies were placing their last coin on these indomitable heights of Cantigny that the French said could not be taken, and if so, could not be held. They had lost, yes hundreds, or even thousands, in attempting what the enemy held as impregnable. Repeatedly did the French attack at this point and repeatedly they were repulsed, only to have their dead rot in the sun, for no one dared attempt to bring them back for burial. Every move was noticed by the enemy. The thick forests were no more, as trees were torn up from their very roots. There now remains only a skeletal forest that offered us no shield as we approached the front lines. These were the conditions as we found them: very shallow trenches, no dug-outs, no first aid stations, no protection for our artillery guns, no barbed wire. Nothing was here as prevailed in the Toul Sector. So our work began.

Saturday, April 27th, the Company was split up into sections—each assigned his task of constructing roads, observation posts, barbed wire entanglements, trenches, dugouts, and first aid stations. I accompanied the section of roadwork. The task consisted of patrolling the road toward the front lines for a distance of five kilometers, filling in all shell holes, and clearing debris from the bombed houses that was scattered all over the roads. The route was traversed twice a day, and twice a day we had to fill in these holes. Some holes were small, but most of them required two and three loads of rock. Many times we were forced to take to the fields to escape the German fire targeted at the road. It was no easy task to recondition these roads. The rock had to be hauled not by wagons, but by cans, buckets, and our hands—all material obtained from the torn down structures.

It was going through the town of Broyes, which we passed through on each trip, that the strain became the greatest. Here we found Company A in a most dangerous position with shells pouring in this town continually and rarely missing human life for which they were intended. Here a shell without exploding tore through the outer covering of a dugout, passed between the legs of a man lying down on an upper bunk, passed through the bunk, through the body of another man lying below, and bored itself through the flooring to the earth beneath. Another shell found its way toward the end of a line of men waiting for supper, killing three, and wounding ten. These are the reports I get when I reply roughly to a word to hurry and get my men out of the town. The statements need no proof for the spots are shown me, and the havoc wrought by these shells is readily seen.

Many times while resting where we think it is safe, we are driven away by the shells striking close, tearing huge holes in the ground and shaking it as though an earthquake was present. For three hours on each trip we hear the ungodly siren of these shells, hearing them before they strike and not knowing where. The suspense is nerve-racking to say the least and a glorious relief when the journey is completed. For miles along the roads is our own artillery camouflaged by the use of wire screens with insertions of grass or green material tied in the screen. This is stretched across the top of the guns allowing only the muzzle of the cannon to protrude. The sense of fear is somewhat alleviated when our artillery is in action, for an enemy shell approaching is not heard, and the only notion of one being on its way is to see it strike. I believe a deaf man is more at ease than another possessing this faculty for the sound of one going through the air is deadly enough.

On one of these trips my section was busy filling in an exceptionally large hole when we heard this dastardly sound of a shell approaching. We were working at a crossroad that we determined was the most dangerous place to be. It seemed to us that the only place this shell could land would be in our midst. As if by command we took to the open field nearby while some Frenchmen were seen running for safety also, when with a crash the explosion came but not too far away to do damage. This shell, as it hummed through the air, echoed through the woods and so distinctly that there was no one near who thought it was not his last time on earth. Yes, I believe a deaf man is more at ease than one with good hearing. However, it was a great joy when, after a week of this duty, I was transferred to some work on another road. I did not envy the section following me on the journey filling up shell holes.

Living History

GENERAL SITUATION ON 1ST DIVISION FRONT[74]

1st Division. A. E. F.,
Le Mesnil-St-Firmin, May 13, 1918.

Telegram
Chief of staff
G. H. 9. A. E. F.

General statement of 1st Division: Coming in contact with the enemy April 25 the division has been in practically a continuous engagement. The infantry has been aggressive and reasonably successful. **The engineers have done very effective work.** The artillery has been active day and night. Total result is German prisoners report that life is very hard for them upon their front, that they no longer can have cooked or hot meals in their two front positions, that they are obliged to keep very close to shelter even far to the rear, the reliefs and evacuation of the wounded are extremely dangerous. Our officers and men are undergoing hardships and losses but sustain them in fine spirits.

ROBERT L. BULLARD.
Major General,
Commanding.

United States Army Center of Military History (1998), "Military Operations of the American Expeditionary Forces," *United States Army in World War I,* version 2, CD-ROM disc 1 of 3, volume IV: 272.

On April 28th the first man of my Company was wounded in this sector. A shell found its way to this fellow's jaw, and he was brought back with many others who were wounded. The hospital units were as busy now as any unit, while each day ambulances loaded with its sickening sights traversed our torn up roads. There was no ceasing of artillery firing from either side; day in and day out we would proceed under this steel arch of shells. To further handicap our work, at night we heard the intermittent droning of the Boche aeroplanes and soon—boom, boom, boom—as the bombs dropped on a nearby town, not knowing when or where the next bombs were going to land. All we knew is the planes were overhead flying around ready with many more bombs.

Finally the order to lay down and keep as close to the ground as possible came. Here we stayed till Fritz[75] relieved himself of his cargo, and we heard the droning of the plane sinking away towards the Boche lines. As the time for going home approached, it was then we realized what a relief to one's nerves this mere thought was. I can tell you there was no time lost in making those five miles back look like one and, ah-h-h, for that bundle of hay and sleep.

April 30th found us resting prior to our departure for another camp in support of the 28th Infantry. Load after load of soldiers, having been wounded at the front, were being driven through our town. Each day had its full count of wounded or killed. Every man became a target for the Boche guns, and no telling when. Barrage after barrage took place with raid after raid, but no retreating. If you could have stood where I was, you would have witnessed the sight of the wounded and dying as they were hurriedly rushed from the trenches. You lay where you were whether at the trenches or five miles behind. You would wonder why a body of men would remain in such a position. But the tide would turn and positions would be reversed.

As we worked between the artillery and front lines, the constant din of artillery fire from the Boche seemed to fade away, when immediately our own artillery sent its answer as counterbarrage. One could understand the attention that was given to the work of our artillery when, as soon as the enemy formed an attack, our guns frustrated their plans with a volley completely demoralizing their ranks; and in an instant there was quietude. This was continual—day in and day out—and there was no opening to allow the enemy to cross our lines. The wounded and dead showed the result of our operation. But one had to remember that the Germans were but forty miles from Paris. Here was the stopping point for the Germans in their mad dash for Paris, and each day now we awaited the renewal of the attack. For two weeks now the enemy had been concentrating its fire on our front lines and back area in its endeavor to drive us back.

On May 4th the order came for departure to our new area. This did not mean rest, but more work—and hard work. After a hike of three kilometers we arrived at a wooded area where my Company pitched tents, provided shelters, and arranged camp in preparation for the remainder of our stay in this area. I with my section was selected for the bowl that was a hollow protected from vision by the trees, and around its edge we dug our shelters. These shelters consisted of holes dug in the bank of the earth with corrugated iron for covering. As a protection from the rain of shrapnel, they were safe, but a shell hitting near by would cave in the shelters and afford no safety whatsoever. It was a case of trust to luck. Many of our long-range guns were emplaced in these woods, and every night the enemy shells would hit around hoping to reach our guns.

As was the custom in our conversations with the French soldiers, we would give all information regarding the sector.[76] No Frenchman could see how we could stop the Germans now from breaking through, and, as to taking the town of Cantigny, they seemed to think it was impossible. While talking to a French soldier, he was endeavoring to tell me something evidently of much interest, but with my little knowledge of the French language, I lost it all. Later I learned that his story was authentic and hinged around a spy who was in our midst. The spy wore an American uniform and rode through our area on trucks picking up valuable information. On one occasion, while passing through the town of Chepoix, a military policeman ordered the truck driver to stop. When the driver refused to obey the order, the military policeman threatened the spy driving the truck, but the truck kept going. The truck was halted and the information the spy had never reached the Germans.

On arrival at our new position, a French artillery officer related how the Germans in their drive for Paris through this point broke through a gap in the lines at the position we now held, but, thinking it was a ruse, retreated. This was also substantiated by the French peasants in the towns around us who were forced to flee during this invasion. I paused here to witness the men badly gassed returning from the front lines. Here they numbered not ten or twenty, but hundreds. A company of infantry that were holding the lines went in with three hundred men but came back with only a hundred. This is hardly believable, but later on as I witnessed this slaughter myself and saw the men in my own Company falling, I doubted nothing and believed everything. However, I found sleep on this night, May 10th, a rare treat in spite of the numerous shells flying overhead. We lay down not with the assurance of an undisturbed slumber, for we knew at any moment we might be called out to support the infantry. An engineer in this war assumed the duties of a doughboy many, many times; so often we discarded the shovel and picked up the rifle.

May 11th was spent in preparation for trench digging at night and awaiting orders. At six o'clock in the evening orders were received for work by the whole Division. The whole regiment of engineers, assisted by the infantry well under the cover of darkness, prepared to take positions along a tapeline extending two thousand feet to the front-line trenches. We were to be ready when ordered to construct a communicating trench as marked off on the tapeline. Well, when darkness came, we were on the move. After hiking four miles, our guides met us. We continued an additional four miles, arriving at a systematically shelled field full of holes.

The night seemed more quiet than was comfortable. It was disturbed occasionally by that terrifying warning of an approaching shell humming overhead only to break in the town behind us, but mighty close to the starting point of our trench. It took a little time to pace off a thousand men along this line of demarcation, all to the impatience of us men, as everyone prayed for the order be given to commence digging so as to get under cover. It was just a night for a wholesale slaughter, and our position was extremely dangerous. As each flare or rocket went up, it was a case of stand perfectly still or lay down. The whole vicinity was lit up like day. Needless to say there was no time lost in digging that six feet of earth away. Each man completed a section of trench three feet long, two feet wide and six feet deep. One can imagine what trying moments it was to be marching in full vision of the Germans to the front-line trench before this first line of communicating trench was dug. Because the trench ran through many of these shell holes, our work was considerably lessened, for many of these shell holes were four and five feet deep. One immediately noticed the completely torn up field with shell holes but two and three feet apart. Evidently many lives were lost going to and from the trenches.

Just before daybreak and at the completion of our work, orders came to leave for camp at the same time a tremendous explosion from a Boche shell hit directly at the beginning or entrance to our trench, killing a captain, a private, and shattering the nerves of a sergeant. The sergeant was found later wandering around in a shell-shocked condition, but he was soon able to relate the incident to official officers, stating that the captain, private, and he on hearing the shell made one dive in the trench. The shell landed between the private and captain, tearing the side out of the captain, killing both immediately. He was uninjured himself. His condition was a pitiful sight, and he was forced to retire to an area back from shell or gunfire.

We were anxious to be on the move and were glad once more to welcome the safe aspect of our shelters back in the woods. We were sent off with a hail of shrapnel and liquid fire striking our front lines and illuminating the area for some distance. This hastened our steps, for it seemed like the first volley of a barrage. We escaped luckily, but we got an idea of how unpleasant our stay in this area was going to be. At daybreak we were in camp, all hands finding joy in sleep. On awakening, orders were ready for us to proceed again to the same position, extending the trench farther back. Again we hiked that eight miles wondering if luck would be with us to-night. Previous to our departure a runner brought word that the line of trench dug last night was horribly damaged by shellfire. We went out again knowing that the Germans were aware of this trench, and visions of their peppering it to-night swept through the ranks.

Well we went to it and soon had our position. The shelling was a little more regular this night, but the distribution was promiscuous. I was watching the infantry crossing the road ready to take their position when a shell tore a hole in their line, killing one man and wounding a number of others. A tremendous shelling soon occurred directly ahead of us—all along the trench we had dug the night before. This forced a delay in our work as there was much gas, necessitating the repeated wearing of our gas masks. However, we worked like beavers, for if the Germans were going to extend their line of fire towards us, we wanted to be under the ground—and deep under, too. We got there and mighty quick. I knew that continual shelling ahead of us would put extra energy into our work. Indeed we had finished and were in camp before the sun thought about rising. This night completed the one-mile of communicating trench to the front lines, and badly did we need it.

On May 16th my Company was ordered to the trenches to construct another communicating trench to the front lines. It was to run along the edge of a woods, or rather what remained of a onetime dense woods, and it was to be the branch of another communicating trench. In the afternoon while making preparations for leaving at 8 o'clock that night, and everyone busy about his little shelter in the hollow in which we camped, a couple of visitors came into our camp dressed in French uniforms, possessing all the insignia of officers. In every way their appearance, manner, and dress would mislead one to believe they were not other than who they pretended to be. They walked about asking various questions, all of which were usual in a matter of conversation. At that time little importance was attached to their presence and was practically forgotten on their departure.

At 8 o'clock the trench tools were distributed, guns and gas masks slung over our shoulders, and helmets adjusted. We set forth, I as usual in the rear of my section. A four-mile hike brought us to the first communication line which we followed for an hour, emerging in the open to a white tapeline which stretched up the side of an incline to the woods and along the outer edge. Along this line as was the custom, we were placed each man three feet apart, ready at a moment's notice to commence digging for all we were worth, for we knew how close the enemy lines were. Even the few shells breaking about were unpleasant, and there was no telling when Fritz would change the range.

We stood for fifteen minutes with hearts pumping like steam engines, praying for the word to dig in, no one seeming to care to talk for fear of awakening Fritz. Then all of a sudden we were shaken, demoralized, and set in a tremendous strain of excitement, for right along this tapeline came the Boche shells, not all hitting at once but one shell following the next. Directly in front of where a fellow and I were standing, a shell landed, and we stood as if paralyzed, listening to the sickening thing burrow its way through the earth. If it exploded, I would not be writing about it now. Without moving, I could have stooped over and picked it up. This shell as a souvenir did not interest me for Fritz was sending them along this line at the rate it seemed of a hundred a minute.

The men on the first volley sought shell holes—five and six of them jumping in one shell hole, while others scattered for the nearest shelter. I lost no time in moving, but unfortunately I chose to move directly in the path of the shells along the tapeline. One shell burst alongside of me sending the big clods of earth all over me, beating at my body. I quickened my steps and ran immediately into another shell bursting and again sending the earth beating at my body. I knew I was going in the wrong direction, for at the end of our line one man lay dead, another severely wounded; guns were taken right off a man's shoulder, not scratching him, and cartridge belts were set on fire by the pieces of shells hitting the cartridges in the belts. At this sight I wavered from my course and took to the gully below followed by others, and from there we watched the slow ebbing of Fritz's anger. I later returned and there found men in all available shell holes hugging the earth as though it was the one God-sent place of safety in all France.

It was but a few minutes when the orders came to get ready to move homeward. This was one command that was readily obeyed, and so at one o'clock, after leaving the dead men in care of the hospital corps and improvising stretchers for the wounded, we left thinking ourselves very fortunate indeed to escape the wholesale slaughter intended for us. With a deep breath of relief, we marched through the trench, arriving at the road where Fritz met us again. Here the Company seemed to automatically scatter, for the first thing I knew, I was in the rear of my section, alone. Our single file line soon wavered, and with the shrapnel bursting overhead, it was difficult to keep the men steady.

We soon learned that we were being followed by shellfire. In front of us a piece of shrapnel killed a horse, and again we changed our course. Still the shells pursued us. Now an airplane was heard overhead and, owing to the bright starlit night, we felt the observer could plainly discern our movements and signal the German artillery. To our right, rockets were going up forming a peculiar signal which we never saw before. We knew they were signals from rockets. Yet it was unusual to see these signals since they were rarely used anywhere but at the front lines, and we were quite a distance from the front lines. We seemed to be getting away from their line of fire when, about a half a mile from camp and our movements unobserved, the shelling ceased.

We had no sooner reached our shelters than Fritz sent a barrage right in the hollow where we were. The man that was brought in from the lines wounded was again wounded; another had his side ripped out so badly that he was also quickly rushed to the hospital. The groaning of this man and the constant roar of shells bursting all about us were extremely uncomfortable. Shells were coming from three different directions, and some never exploded but landed on top of shelters where men had just entered.

I was called from my precarious position and ordered to take the men to the field where a trench had been dug. This I did, but the shelling of this trench drove us out and to a town three miles back. Here we spent the rest of the morning. We had to see an officer from my Company who was in charge of the engineer supplies in this town in order to have the military police allow us to leave the town. In talking to him it just dawned upon me that the shelling of our shelters was done through spy work, and the two visitors in our camp yesterday dressed as French officers were nothing else but German spies in French uniforms.

At 11 o'clock we arrived back to camp but not at all eager to enter that hollow again. That was the first and last time that hollow was shelled, and never through the whole war had that place been touched before. On inspection of the hollow we found that our camp was all battered up, especially the kitchen area. The big twenty-gallon water tank was plugged full of holes, and one coffee boiler was put out of commission. As we needed water, it necessitated a drive of two hours to the next town. Our dinner was considerably delayed. As a matter of fact, Fritz had done a good job.

This night we were treated to a layoff, so all hands were in bed early. My sleep was interrupted at 2:00 a.m. I was called to hike to the trenches with a detail and officer in charge to construct a first aid station. This march was just before daybreak so Fritz could not observe us coming. Our point at the lines was a good five-mile walk—all the way through shellfire. First we kept to the road which was badly torn up. On approaching the village of Villers-Tournelle, which was constantly under surveillance by the Germans and being shelled continually, we took to the fields, keeping well out from the town. We walked along the edge of a woods at the outskirts of Villers-Tournelle. While crossing the fields, we could see the balls of fire as the shrapnel broke at the crossroads in the town. All troops were cautioned to avoid the intersections of roads. No man was allowed to traverse the roads alone, and when with another, was told to keep five paces apart.

We were now ready to descend to Deathman's Valley, one through which all our troops must go in order to get to the lines unobserved. We were fully aware of this ghastly valley where many lives were lost trying to go through—and we were not to miss the shelling either. Fritz timed us wrong, however, and the shelling which was directly in our path fell short, yet near enough to make all men dive for shell holes or lay down. We were soon up double timing across the valley as machine gun bullets passed overhead. Quickly we reached the edge of a steep incline which afforded the shelter we desperately needed, and with much relief we awaited our instructions. We were to dig into the side of this incline six feet, cover the top with corrugated iron, and use brush as camouflage.

As the hill was thick with foliage and difficult for the German artillery to reach, we felt rather secure in our working. A tremendous bombardment of our communicating trench drew our attention to the valley, and from our station we watched the Germans unmercifully shell this trench as infantry was marching through. One shell broke directly in the trench sending clods of dirt and human limbs clean over the parapet. We were forced to get under shelter from the flying pieces of shells which would batter at the iron coverings lying about. All day this valley had a large number of shells sent into it, and all these shells were breaking within fifty to a hundred yards of us. All we knew was we must go through this valley on leaving.

At 8:30 our relief came, and this commenced our attempt to hike five miles back to camp. We got through the valley just in time, for Fritz had our journey mapped out and shelled behind us. At intense moments as these, one automatically walked afraid to breathe and ignorant to everything except the "powey" of those Capt. [cent] *Cinquante-Cinqs*.[77] The next spot of worry was the village of Villers-Tournelle and adjacent woods. We were able to avoid the shelling as we passed through the town, but in the woods we caught it. Over our heads the shells sang, but the accompaniment was our feet double timing over the hills. For two months the feeling of being continually in the jaws of death was enough to skeletonize our beings. Can you wonder why 160-lb. men weighed 100 pounds?

May 19: The dawn of a new day found the German and our own artillery in a duel—a constant roar of guns all day. Again and again we made this five-mile tramp to the trenches, starting at 8 o'clock at night and being relieved at 2:30 p.m. All means possible were used to hasten the completion of these aid stations, and even now before completion severely wounded men were brought in to receive shelter and attention prior to being sent across this hellhole to a hospital. Shelling was heavy all night at the front lines resulting in many casualties, and still men were passing us on their way to and from the trenches. While time drew near for our departure, Fritz seemed to increase his shelling of the valley. He knew men were going through this valley, and hence every five minutes he shelled the area.

During one of these pauses we availed ourselves of the opportunity to go and go quickly; in this manner we beat his shellfire but often not any too soon. Once back at camp, orders awaited me to change my time and take my detail out at 2:30 in the morning, working till 9:00 in the evening.

On May 21st we had opportunity to witness a few of the many air battles staged at this sector. Our work at the first aid dugout was now done during the day but completely unobserved from the enemy trenches or artillery. Many times we would cease work to watch the anti-aircraft guns in action. We were intensely absorbed in seeing the German aeroplanes maneuver through the air as shrapnel after shrapnel would explode what seemed but a few feet from their target, and then we would find the planes emerge from this barrage sometimes unharmed and sometimes gradually descending towards their lines in flames.

Often times the muffled sound of machine guns in action would attract our attention to the air, and we would watch the many battles among French, American, and German fliers. There would be as many as ten and fifteen planes maneuvering about in anticipation of catching their opponents at a disadvantage; one or two planes would be seen falling, and soon the rest would disperse. These battles usually took place near the lines, and many disabled planes landed safely in their own territory unless the loss of control of the plane prevented this. On one occasion a German plane fell in no-man's-land. The pilot was safely rescued by the Germans.

On no other front were aeroplanes so active in the daytime. They became a big factor in directing artillery fire and in observing. It appeared the Germans were well-informed of the intensive operations behind our lines with the help of aeroplanes and their spy system. But, based on our success, the information they carried back to German headquarters was of little assistance to them.

At ten o'clock in the morning on that first day of work, while I was in charge of two aid stations under completion with six men working on each, I noticed an aeroplane hovering about overhead. Its continual circling directly over our location was in itself of great significance, for soon a tremendous bombardment along the slope where we were working drove us all inside, closely hugging the walls. Shells began to break thick and fast, tearing trees down, causing them to fall over our shelters. Pieces of shell were falling inside our shelter, one of which I picked up immediately on landing and found it too hot to hold. Things were becoming too uncomfortable after ten minutes of such suspense, so I ordered all men out and made a dash for a certain dugout near by. This bombardment I knew was centered on our shelters. With the rain of shells pouring in all about us, I thought they would soon make a hit, and the covering we had would be torn away and men with it.

Again the plane was directing the fire, so I lost no time in acting. When one shell seemed to tear up the whole slope and send it in on us, I started my first man out. He hesitated, for pieces of shell were showering heavily around. He made a dash down a different slope followed by another man until one dugout was clean. Then I trusted to Providence and dashed for the next shelter. None of these men seemed anxious to leave but wanted to trust to luck. However, I got them started, and all hands took the leap for life. Fritz seemed to be working fast, too. I followed but didn't go to the dugout, for the closeness of the shells drove me into a little shelter in which an infantryman was closely huddled up; and there I waited. Here a whole company of infantry had holes dug into a slope below our work and apparently safe from shells. All along here, however, pieces of shells would land as the bombardment continued on the aid stations. The shelling continued for twenty minutes after we left, so I had visions of completely demolished shelters on our return.

After Fritz subsided, I returned with the men and found everything intact with a little extra covering over the top. With that half-hour bombardment the nearest hit was eight feet away. We welcomed the relief and were glad to get away from this area for a few hours, but now we had to face the hard grind homeward. Each day the shelling increased while places that were once safe, now were shelled in turn. Our motto became "trust to luck and all that's holy." Everyday mutilated doughboys were brought by on stretchers, the bearers necessarily traversing the valley to hasten attention to their wounded.

On May 23rd the work was about completed on our aid stations with the exception of a few timbers for the roof to protect the shelters from pieces of shells. I detailed a few men to go up the slope and cut these timbers. Fritz was shelling about considerably but confined his attention to the valley below. Unexpectedly he sent a few shells along the slope where we were. Immediately my anxiety for the men at work there was increased, when all of a sudden one of them yelled. I presumed someone was hit. Soon they all came down, and on questioning the yelling, I learned the exclamation arose from the nearness of the explosion that sent a piece of shrapnel flying that cut the bottom button off the jacket of one of the men—a lucky escape from a nasty slice. Many can boast of just such narrow escapes as this fellow had this day. Despite the shelling, the work was completed. Because Fritz was well-informed of this work and did considerable shelling around it each day, we were decidedly in favor of something else.

On May 24th I received orders to construct aid stations at the front line, so I took my detail through the gauntlet to the front lines where the dangers presented themselves in a variety of forms. In the first place the Boche were using no discrimination in dispersing their shells around and especially favoring the communicating trenches to the front lines. On passing through these trenches, we found the parapet at different intervals was caved in from high explosives, which compelled us to all but crawl along, shielding ourselves from German snipers that were ever watchful for the sight of a helmet rising above the trench. The familiar sound of rifle bullets passing overhead did not worry us, but the dread of a siren as a six-inch shell approached was a source of great concern. Once while going through and once on returning we were forced to climb to the top in order to allow the wounded being carried to the rear to pass by.

On reaching the front lines we found the trenches in better condition, but the stench of dead bodies was a sickening odor. These were bodies of French, Moroccan, and Algerian soldiers who had been lying in the woods behind our front lines for weeks; there was no opportunity to give them a proper burial. We accustomed ourselves to these conditions, and work progressed with little notice of this ill-scented odor. I found a few minutes to chat with the infantry who were holding the lines. On asking them what the French thought of this sector when they were being relieved, one sergeant told of conversation he had with a Frenchman who remained in the lines after his Company, the Blue Devils,[78] was relieved. This remaining fellow put a knife between his teeth and jumped over the top with a word that he was going to get one more Dutchman[79] before leaving. A half-hour later the Frenchman returned for his equipment and was asked if he got him. He smiled and said, "Good-night," and off he went.

I was also informed a raid is started by the Dutchmen on an average of four times a week—sometimes at daybreak, but mostly at night. For the three days we worked out there, only once did the Dutchmen start over. We had to take our places with the infantry, cease work, and quickly. Machine guns commenced action that resulted in a slaughter of the Germans at the front lines as they were getting out of their trench. That was as far as they got, and we cannot say we were sorry. The French still claimed we would never hold Cantigny if taken, saying the German positions were too well-fortified behind the town. No one as yet knew when the attack was to take place, but preparations were hurried through. A doughboy near me was eating rations unfamiliar to me. On questioning him, he told me of the dead bodies in the woods behind us. He said that many of the infantry would crawl out to these dead bodies and find equipment for themselves such as trench tools, knives, pistols, and gas masks; and they got three- and four-day rations from these dead. A couple of my men crawled over on their bellies in the morning, but returned with nothing but a sickened heart.

On May 26th we were completing our work as ordered by our captain.[80] Owing to the orders that all such work was to cease today, it was important that the shelters were finished before leaving. Three men thought they would facilitate the construction of these shelters by working on top where apparently they were shielded by thick brush. They were progressing rapidly when their location was observed by one of Fritz's snipers. A rain of machine gun bullets pattering about our place of operation aroused me to think something was amiss.

I hurried from where I was giving instructions on another shelter and met one of my men who informed me Fritz made a hit. Hurrying to their shelter I found one fellow with three nasty bullet wounds, while the other two fellows were hugging the ground with Fritz peppering away in their vicinity. They fell down inside and escaped another fusillade[81] of Boche lead. These three fellows were standing shoulder to shoulder working when Fritz spied them, but only one was wounded; the other two ducked in time. One of these fellows for the second time narrowly escaped a wooden cross: the first time he was the one who had the button from his jacket cut clean by a piece of shrapnel, marking a slight bruise on his stomach. This same fellow later on, however, had his side torn out, resulting in his almost immediate death.

Our troubles started now in getting this wounded lad through the trenches. After trying to carry a stretcher through this narrow passageway and progressing slowly, we were forced to take to the top[82] in order to allow troops coming in and going out to pass. It was quite dark now with the Boche artillery very active. I was elected to return for the fellow's equipment; hence, I lost my party and now had to make it back to camp alone. It was an uncomfortable passage through the trench owing to the heavy shellfire around, with shells breaking first behind, then in front; and the appearance of this shell-torn trench increased my anxiety. It was usually the Boche's policy to shell heavily when they expected reliefs to take place, and this was one of the times they appeared to know.

On leaving the trench I caught up with the tail end of another engineering party being relieved while troops were also passing us going into the trench. Fritz had one barrage for us with the usual sound of a siren followed by deadly explosions, causing the men in front of me to throw themselves down on the ground. I hurdled them, for I did not care to stop till I crossed that valley. I left this party and, after debating which was the best route for me, I met some men from my Company and inquired of them which way the wounded lad was taken. They pointed out the dangerous yet quickest path across the valley. I wished to catch up to them if possible, so I made a double-quick step through the valley and up the slope just escaping what I expected—a concentrated fire in the valley.

On reaching the slope a company of infantry was hurrying along, and in the rear of this outfit I followed. I felt relieved a bit, for, if wounded, there was aid; but when alone, there is nothing but the stars to offer sympathy. I had no sooner gotten under way with this Company than a shell split the line. I knew now that my feet were not moving fast enough, so I left the rear and started ahead. The ghastly sound of a siren halted me. The approaching shell exploded along the slope, but ahead. I soon passed that spot and reached the road leading to that dreaded of all places, Villers-Tournelle. I made up my mind after plodding along the road with no one to talk to but the Boche—and they could not even hear what I was saying to them—to take a chance on dead man's crossing, trusting and praying that Fritz would keep quiet till I got through the town.

On the outskirts a dead doughboy was lying covered over with a blanket with the blood still streaming down the road. This sight was anything but pleasant on such a night, so with eyes glued on that town and crossroads, expecting the usual bursting of shrapnel to intensify my feelings, I plied on as in a trance. I passed through the town and was safe on the direct road to camp. All of a sudden a tremendous barrage took place at the front lines. Fritz was making a raid. The shells began to break in the town, and for three miles I listened to and watched shells exploding in the woods to my left—after they passed over my head. I knew their target was the road, but their range was fortunately imperfect. I left the road anyway and proceeded along the field parallel to the road at a distance of fifty feet, for if Fritz was aiming for the road, he might make a mistake and hit it.

Gas explosions became evident, so as the Lord helps them that help themselves, and He sure was helping me this night, I donned my mask. I wore the mask until I could not get sufficient air in my lungs since my heart was beating overtime as it was. I took the mask off and made for the road again as a truck was hitting it at a lively pace. I waylaid the truck and welcomed with open arms a human being at last! This truck missed two explosions going through Villers-Tournelle, barely escaping wreckage. A man from my Company was inside and had been crossing the fields to Villers-Tournelle when the barrage started, saying that the gas was unbearable there and that the shelling behind him was so dense that everyone must be hemmed in.

We reached camp in safety and learned the next morning that two hundred doughboys were being taken to the hospital along with seventeen of my Company who were gassed in this attack. There was no abatement to the shelling of back areas, so during the day we were busy ducking from tree to tree in our hollow as pieces of high explosives and shrapnel would rain in on us. There were artillery pieces in the town of Mesnil that were

Living History

CANTIGNY AFFAIR EMPHASIZES IMPORTANCE OF ORGANIZING OUR OWN DIVISIONS AND HIGHER UNITS[83]

General Headquarters, A.E.F.

No. 1223-S   Chaumont, Haute-Marne, June 1, 1918

The Adjutant General, Washington, D.C.

Personal and confidential for Chief of Staff and Secretary of War

While relatively small, the affair at Cantigny on the 28th was well planned and splendidly executed. The 28th Infantry under Colonel Hanson Ely made the attack supported by our artillery and several additional batteries of heavy guns specially sent to the sector for the purpose. Our infantry reached its objective in schedule time and immediately organized its new position. It was important in this first attack that we should succeed and that we should hold our ground, especially as the French had previously taken Cantigny twice and had each time been driven out by the Germans. Under my personal direction additional troops of the 18th and 26th were at once brought up to support the line. Five strong counterattacks were made by the Germans all of which were dissipated, leaving prisoners in our hands. Our staff work was excellent and the liaison perfect. Twenty minutes after the new position was reached the information was at divisional headquarters; soon thereafter telephone communication was established and maintained. The Allies are high in praise of our troops. This action illustrates the facility with which our officers and men learn, and **emphasizes the importance of organizing our own divisions and higher units** as soon as circumstances permit. It is my firm conviction that our troops are the best in Europe and our staffs are the equals of any.

PERSHING.

United States Army Center of Military History (1998), "Policy-forming Documents of the American Expeditionary Forces," *United States Army in World War I*, version 2, CD-ROM disc 1 of 3, volume II: 434.

only one hundred yards away from where we were working. These artillery pieces were evidently worrying the Boche considerably. Fritz sent his aeroplanes over to locate this artillery. Later on they sent their shells over trying to break up this source of concern to them, so continuing through the whole day we kept pretty much under shelter as shell after shell exploded. This night seemed to be time off for artillery action and raids at our sector; however, we knew the night was not passing without its usual raids, for the continual roaring of the British guns to the left of Montdidier was distinctly heard for twenty minutes.

At daybreak on May 27th, the day before our planned attack on Cantigny, the Boche attempted again to penetrate our lines and gain information. During the heavy barrage impostors who posed as an officer with two doughboys in attendance tried to demoralize the infantry by ordering the trenches vacated and for all to retreat in small groups over a hill. This hill, let me tell you, was being unmercifully shelled with shrapnel, high explosives, gas, and what was known as golden rain.[84] However, fortunately the order was not obeyed and Fritz was repulsed, leaving the greater part of the raiding party in no-man's-land. The officer was not seen again that day, or the day after, or perhaps he went back to Germany. This night was a restless one for all with the expectation of the battle in the morning and wondering what part we each would play when the curtain rises at daybreak or zero hour—five o'clock.

It was the night before, yes, and a still night—no artillery action, just a lull before a storm. Not a suspicion of the tragedy to follow dampened the apparent joy existing among the troops. The eagerness for action with which we all were ready kept us strung to a high pitch of excitement. Not an explosion was heard, as if the artillery division was busy oiling its machinery and cleaning the very muzzles of every gun. The intermittent droning of a Boche plane disturbed the peacefulness of the night as though warning the troops of a gruesome calamity being staged before us. This droning was meant to signal that the Germans were ready to meet our advance; it bespoke but an omen of success, for it meant uneasiness to the evident restlessness among the German officers.

For a month now a setting had been planned and worked out. First we observed the vast amount of artillery placed in woods and behind hedges and secreted in torn down villages. Even to the second line of defense were they set, lined up in skirmish order, ready to give and take, till the bore of the artillery melted away or a hostile shell tore it from its foundation. Joking and laughter died down to supreme quietude as the approach to the lines was near. Only the constant patter of the horses' hoofs could be heard, as with untiring haste they strained upon the chains secured to their heavy burdens. The huge tanks with guns protruding like an octopus sent their welcome to the doughboys in the front lines, bucking all obstacles as they hastened to their position in the valley. The D Company of the Engineers was chosen to accompany the infantry on their expedition. This unit was concentrated on the slope leading to the front lines where they would take their places. When the order for over the top was sounded, they were to be part of the first wave of infantry along with the tanks. The balance of the engineer forces was held at their post, ready at a moment's notice to take positions in case of an unsubdued counterattack, or to replace the ranks depleted by wounded or dead...*for Cantigny must be taken.*

You can imagine the nervous strain when at 4:30 a.m. the order speedily went through the trenches to load and fix bayonets. The peacefulness reigning through the whole night was soon to awaken amid a deluge of steel, fire, and merciless destruction of human life. At 4:45 a.m. we began to watch for that one signal, that one rocket that towers above the rest, calling to arms not only our men but every being around, in front of us or in back of us, to the right or to the left, calling every piece of machinery to action from the front lines to positions ten miles behind. "We're off!" was the only exclamation heard as the signal for destruction went up. As though one touch operates the hundreds of cannons around, the timely but deadly barrage was there to greet the infantry, as hastily they went up and over. The huge tanks spit forth their incessant fire as they pushed on, over the torn up field of no-man's-land. The waves of infantry as they crossed no-man's-land were seen in orderly fashion, but soon crowded together, joking and laughing. Soon the Boche were seen hurrying from their trenches and offered no resistance. The infantry in double time sent a volley of fire and advanced beyond the town, forcing the Germans to retire beyond their artillery.

The town was taken with many prisoners, and the order was given to dig in. The Germans surviving the attack immediately called their artillery to action and poured their deadly fire on our troops as they endeavored to get under the ground. One man all but finished digging a hole when a shell caved it in. Again he worked only to have another shell cave it in. Three times was he forced to urge his tiring muscles to the task. An officer on seeing one of his men shot down by a sniper, jumped from his improvised trench, with pistol raised, but met the fate of the one he tried to avenge. A group of Boche captured beyond their front lines were being lined up prior to being sent to headquarters when one became unruly. The sergeant knocked him down. In German, the soldier said, "You don't know you struck a woman, do you?" She was dressed as an officer and was sent along separately.

Carrier pigeons sent from the front lines informed all in the rear that Cantigny was taken. An aeroplane viewing the attack periodically returned to headquarters dropping messages, keeping all posted as to the success. First words were the German front line was taken, next the woods were captured with many prisoners, and then Cantigny with its dominating heights had fallen. The infantry went beyond its objective and was forced to retire a little. Next came word that the infantry was digging in amidst a torrent of shells and gas. For three hours the heavy cannonading continued. Only when the infantry was well dug in did the Germans gather their forces together and, in a well-directed blow, let fly a volley of shells that shook the very dome of the sky. They made a vicious onslaught on our lines but were repulsed with heavy losses. Again and again they attempted to regain their position only to retire with losses predominating. On the morning of May 30th for four hours the Boche sent over their deadly gas shells, following this up with another attack on our positions; but their attempt was futile. Their last hope had vanished. Quietude now reigned for the rest of the day.

On May 31st I was sent out to clean up around the old front lines, making a salvage pile of rifles, belts, gas masks, and various articles of equipment. I took interest in viewing the old German front lines where the trenches were a litter of shell holes, damaged beyond any semblance of a safe place to stay. Tape was laid from our old front line to the Germans old front line preparatory to digging a communicating trench. No-man's-land was nothing but shell holes, and its appearance showed how deadly the land was between the two lines. That evening the usual work details were sent out to construct the trenches. The following night I was assigned as guide to conduct a party to a position selected for a post command where a dugout would be constructed. At 1:30 a.m. we set out on this rather unpleasant assignment, for that town of ill omen (Villers-Tournelle) had to be crossed. Since the German range on this town was reduced, owing to the taking of Cantigny, we did not experience much shelling as we passed through the town. However, a few gas shells pursued me as I left my party. Hesitating going through the town, I made a detour and took to the outskirts.

On June 5th all the work pursued by my Company was ordered stopped. Word came for the Company to prepare a position which was to the left of our present camp and three kilometers from a town called Coullemelle. This camp consisted of a large brick barn with various buildings attached forming a quadrangle, of which the central part was decorated with a huge manure pile. The significance of the manure pile was little thought about till the following morning when the present owners drove up with their country team of horses and, after thrusting about a bit, extricated bottles and bottles of that luscious *vin rouge* and *vin blanc*.[85] Here we had a café on our premises, but closed to visitors. The French peasants lost no time in loading the wine into the wagon; however, many bottles were sold in the process. From our present location work began in constructing fortifications and in strengthening our positions. It was surmised that the next German attack was to be made through our defenses, as the Germans were naturally bitter by the loss of Cantigny and advantageous surroundings.

At 9:30 p.m. on June 6th our first call to the alert sounded, and we hastily took positions in the third-line trenches where we remained till 6:30 in the morning. We were entertained all night by the constant roar of artillery firing. At four o'clock in the morning the Germans attempted a surprise attack but were forced to retire back to their trenches, being completely repulsed by the 28th Infantry. At 6:30 we returned to camp—tired, wet, and hungry. The day was given to resting up, but at 9 p.m. orders were received to construct a barbed wire entanglement in front of the artillery positions in Coullemelle. Cheered by hopes of a peaceful move, we marched forth, hearing nothing but that intermittent droning of the Boche planes bent on some bombing tour. As expected the bombs came, not at us but two hundred yards to our left; the French with vast amounts of artillery were the targets. These artillery positions were so placed that an enemy shell under no circumstances could do damage, so Fritz conceived the plan of sending his bombers out to foster a habitual source of worriment. However, our fear was the fact that the bombs often missed their mark by 200 yards, so we were kept in a somewhat nervous strain till Fritz gave the job up and said "good-night."

At ten o'clock the system we were to use to install the barbed wire entanglement was told to all, and I found myself in charge of the carrying squad. My men would bring the stakes, another squad would hammer them in the ground, and still another squad would run the wire. This line of barbed wire extended from Coullemelle to Villers-Tournelle, a distance of a mile. Off the road about twenty-five yards was another section of the Company constructing a trench, while our work lay in the other side of the road toward the front-line trenches. We had been working pretty fast, so we figured there were enough stakes to keep the other squad busy; hence, the men in my detail lay down to rest along the edge of the road in random fashion. Things were exceptionally quiet—not an artillery gun could be heard, although the artillery was massed just in back of our place of working. We could hear orders given by the officers and occasionally words spoken. I was pacing up and down the road strangely absorbed in the stillness of the night, and I could not shake from my mind the thought of a disastrous end to it all.

Soon a man approached me. "Sergeant," he said, "one of our Company fell asleep. Here, I'll show you." He took me down the road a way, and there half out in the road and half way on the grass was the form of one sound asleep. "Wake him up when it's time to go in, will you?" He left with the assurance I would, and then I thought what a calamity to this young fellow if an urgent call came. I felt sure something was going to happen. My watch said 12:15—nothing usually happens at this time. Still uneasy, I started back to get my detail in line for more stakes, and as I came to my rifle and belt that lay on the ground, I stopped and hesitatingly put on my belt and slung my rifle over my shoulder.

"I know something is going to happen," I thought. I reached the first of my men still lying on the ground when explosions, shells, dirt, and stakes came upon us. Stunned as I was to this sudden barrage, I saw a shell explode in the midst of a group of men getting ready to place a stake. Groans, curses and maledictions followed. Men scurried here, there, and everywhere in search of shelter from the constant hail of shells. One ball exploded alongside of me, throwing pieces of shell over me, only to roll off my arm. I knew someone was hit, so I shouted, "Anyone hit?" One said, "I'm hit." Another said, "I'm hit."

I laid down my gun to give first aid when the two spoke up and said they could walk to the trench if I would lead them. Immediately I grabbed one by an arm and the other by his arm and started across the road. Battered and hammered from all angles, we reached the trench, and I threw one of the soldiers one way, and the other another way, and took an Annette Kellerman[86] myself in and on top of a fellow. The trench was so shallow it barely covered him, so I had to speedily edge in alongside somehow but was forced to expose half of my body. Here we lay hemmed in from all sides. How we got across the road through that hail of steel, God knows. As each shell struck closely, I could feel the form beneath me double up. At the same time I would also do the same and clutch at the earth, praying as I never prayed before.

Through this shallow trench a figure was crawling, whom I found to be the gas officer. I stopped him wondering where he was going through such an intense bombardment. He crouched next to me, and there he anchored. Soon I began to sniff fumes of gas and asked if we had not better sound the gas alarm. "Not bad enough," he said. The continuous fumes were a warning, so we gave the word for masks on, shouting as loud as we could, and at the same time donning our own. We lost no time in putting these masks on and getting our helmets back on our heads, for pieces of shells were flying thickly. For some reason or other the gas NCO[87] could not find his helmet after adjusting his mask. He inquired, "Where's my helmet?" and started feeling for mine. "Look out. This is not yours," I said, as he grabbed for mine. Still the shells kept coming. "Get your helmet, Man." Again he grabbed for mine, and a third time he tried to get mine. I now felt around, and by my feet there his helmet lay.

How long after this shelling we hugged the ground we do not know, but word came to file out. Crawling along on our bellies, we reached a place of vantage and in single file marched across the fields, striking directly for the farmhouse and home. We arrived there at 2:30 a.m. and were immediately called to the alert position, occupying the third line. Shells were breaking directly ahead of us, wounding many men. A gradual cessation of artillery fire relieved us at 12:30 p.m. that day, and very glad we were to get away. It rained continually the whole day, so wet, sore, and hungry we marched to camp in small detachments.

The following day found me on the job, constructing a post command under the road between Villers-Tournelle and Rocquencourt. During our work here we were witnesses to much shellfire on the town of Villers-Tournelle and concentrated gas fire on Coullemelle. Like a steam engine these gas shells would follow one behind another, exploding as each one took its place in the town. The fumes were penetrating to our post, necessitating wearing the gas mask for fifteen minutes until the shelling finally waned. An infantryman passing stopped for a chat and informed us that a Boche was found concealed in a shell hole and had been there for three days now, since the taking of Cantigny. He asked why the Germans had not retaken this town, as his reason for remaining concealed was that he knew he would be rescued soon when the town was retaken. He was escorted back as a prisoner and informed that Cantigny would never be occupied by the Germans again. Another batch of prisoners wanted to know where the three-inch machine guns were located. Owing to the rapid fire of our artillery, it was not surprising that the prisoners thought it was a machine gun; but they had to be convinced that we as yet had no machine gun shooting a three-inch shell.

The excitement over the capture of Cantigny had abated,[88] and now work to strengthen our positions began in earnest. At night we frequently heard the Boche planes and the usual load of bombs sent down. On one night the bombing became so intense near us that all were ordered in the dugout that was under construction under a barn. Soon we were back to slumber again only to awake and be notified of the usual work at hand. A detail on returning from the lines heard one of the German planes approaching, and all sought shelter from probable shell pieces. When the plane had passed over their heads, they started their journey homeward. They had just entered the road when a shell exploded. Later one of the detail cried, "I'm hit." Hurrying over, we found his arm all but completely severed from his body. His injury required a handkerchief and tourniquet to tighten the rag and stop the flow of blood. His life was saved, and after months at the hospital he was sent home, but died from the prevalent disease influenza.

On June 12th I was sent out on one of the relief assignments to construct a dugout in Rocquencourt for the commanding officer Colonel Ely of the

28th Infantry. It was a veritable underground home consisting of sleeping quarters, smoking room, kitchen, and air shaft. The cornerstone bearing the name of Co. F can be seen there now. During the building of this dugout we were completely unobserved by enemy planes and observation balloons, having stretched camouflage above us. As I was on the day shift, there was much opportunity to witness frequent air battles with many planes being brought down on both sides. While doing a night shift on this dugout, I had an occasion to be near the Colonel's room during a barrage staged by the Germans. An artillery officer in consultation with him asked, "Colonel, shall I send over a few?" "Yes, you might as well," the Colonel replied. Soon he was giving orders over the telephone which resulted in a young barrage.[89] Then things settled down to a peaceful night. When we were relieved, the bombers came out, striking hard at the French artillery nearby.

As a divergence from the hard grind of six weeks on the Cantigny front, June 16th was a day of relief enjoyed by all members of the 1st Division. We had a baseball game followed by an open-air vaudeville performance which was held behind the lines. Fortunately we were unobserved by the enemy although within range of their big guns. We were soon back in camp at the conclusion of all performances, and there we eagerly read the evening edition of the newspaper relating to the Austrian and Italian offensive where the drive was being pursued by the Italians with much success. On June 20th the work on the dugout near Villers-Tournelle was completed, so we were sent to Rocquencourt for underground construction of dugouts.

On the night of June 21st, after a three-day lapse in hostilities, the Boche directed heavy artillery fire on our positions supervised by aeroplanes, which paved the way for heavy barrages from our anti-aircraft guns. Hence the night was considerably livelier with artillery, bombing planes, and anti-aircraft guns in action. The Boche now seemed to be warming up to something, so immediate preparations started for defending our position against any sudden attack. It was the belief that Germany was contemplating an offensive through our territory, so to meet the emergency each company of engineers sent a detachment for schooling in how to handle a machine gun. A week's training was sufficient for them, while speed was in vogue on all work at the lines.

On June 28th at 2:30 in the afternoon, while superintending some work outside of the dugout, a tremendous machine gun barrage took place, coming from all points of the surrounding fields. A glance upward was sufficient to acquaint one with the why of it all. Boche aeroplanes were reaping a harvest from observations, but the intense barrage soon caused them to journey homeward. Our observation balloons were taking advantage of the clear day, and hence a number of these were up, and but a few hundred yards behind us. We could see these balloons clear from the English sector, forming the shape of the Western Front for miles. The German balloons were also easily seen. Much interest, however, was centered on groups of aeroplanes as they swiftly flew towards the balloons for a shot that would destroy them.

I was glancing towards the German lines when, as far as was visible, a plane, though a speck in the distance, gradually became larger and larger. It was coming directly towards us. I still watched it, and without wavering one bit, it reached our lines, when all machine guns in the vicinity let fire at it. Still it came on a direct course, speeding at a low altitude. More guns opened up on it from every surrounding spot, eager to bring man and machine down. The barrage was terrific, but still undaunted the aeroplane sailed over our heads, making directly for the balloon behind us. A form was seen jumping from the balloon, his parachute opening, leading the observer to safety, while a shot set his balloon on fire. The Boche, skillfully circling the balloon, commenced his daring rush homeward through the same barrage of machine gun and rifle fire, passing through the gauntlet, reaching the lines apparently unharmed. To our right three other Boche planes attempted the same trick, but failed. A battle between our planes and the Boche resulted in the bringing down of one of the enemy and scattering the remaining two planes.

The excitement to say the least was intense for a time. Behind it all, however, I had visions of a strenuous attack soon approaching. At night there was an unusual demonstration of bombing, and continually the explosions were heard, driving us to our dugout under our quarters. A heavy artillery barrage at daybreak had us up with full equipment, waiting for possible orders to proceed to the lines. We later learned from a hospital worker that the Germans sent a heavy barrage over on our lines five minutes before the 26th Infantry was to go over on a raid. Our barrage opened up and, strictly to orders, the 26th Infantry went over the top through the barrage of the Germans, captured prisoners and returned to the amazement of the

Dutchmen, who could not understand how men would go through the fire of the Germans unless they were crazy.

On Monday, July 1st, we were called to the trenches, reaching the third line at twelve o'clock at night, where we spent that night up until nine o'clock in the morning. Fritz was very busy with bombs, but we kept low. At twelve o'clock, July 3rd, the Americans and French artillery opened up with all guns. We had visions of an attack that would cause us to be called again to the trenches. This did not happen for we learned the round of artillery was a salute of forty-eight guns—one for each state—in celebration of the 4th of July. We went to Varmaise where the holiday was devoted to amusements of all sorts. While in Varmaise I engaged in a conversation with a Frenchman who spoke of the everlasting grind of the War. He was very discouraged and thought there was no end to it. [Ed. Congratulations for the Cantigny success are recorded in General Order 24, which is included in the Appendix: 151. Soldiers of the First Division were awarded the Victory Medal[90] for their participation in the Storming of Cantigny, Appendix: 152.]

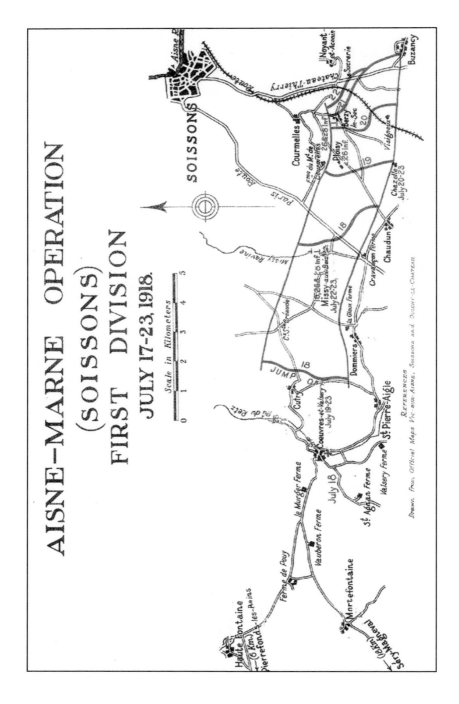

Figure 12: Map of Aisne-Marne (Soissons) Campaign[91]

AISNE-MARNE OPERATION

On July 7th we received orders to leave camp at 11 p.m. As we prepared to depart, we were relieved by a company of French engineers. At twelve o'clock with full equipment we set out, hiking twelve kilometers to a village called Froissy, two kilos from Noyers-Saint-Martin, arriving there at 5 a.m. Many of us were foot-sore and weary after spending the whole night on the road, so we were soon pitching tents. On July 9th we set out again at 5 a.m., hiking another twelve kilos to a town called Sauqueuse-Saint-Lucien, arriving there at 9 a.m. We pitched our tents in a field. Here the first indications of a long rest pointed our way when orders came to turn in our gas masks and helmets, and the first passes to visit other towns were issued to a great number of the Company. Well-satisfied with our lot now, we prepared for a long stay of mirth and pleasure. The village of Beauvais with a population of 30,000 was the center of attraction. As the whole Division was centered in this area, the town was kept quite lively. Beauvais had its celebration for the first time during the War.

On July 12th the brightness suddenly changed to a dark and gloomy despair when orders came to entrain immediately, and our gas masks and helmets were handed back to us. You can imagine our disappointment. Rumor had it that the Germans were driving hard on the Champagne front. True to orders we loaded equipment and left at ten o'clock on the morning of the 13th. This was not a hike, as we were packed in trucks for an all night ride. Each man was trying to sleep on the other fellow's shoulder. As we passed through the outskirts of Paris at 8:30 a.m., we could see where a few of the shells from the long-range guns of the Boche tore down dwellings. At

9 a.m. we arrived in Roissy, the largest town of any in which we had been. However, the 1st Division was not to enjoy this town, for at 7 p.m., July 15th, we left again in a convoy of trucks, packed in like sardines. It was almost a court-martial offense to take space for one's feet, so, after all got seated, we tangled all our feet in a bunch, and thereby made room for our packs, helmets, gas masks, and guns.

The night was spent in misery, and what was worse, no one knew where the Division was heading. We asked the Frenchmen who were driving the trucks, and they informed us it was Chateau-Thierry. We let it go at that. It was a dark, chilly night, and we had no lights lit on our truck. Unfortunately we had engine trouble and lost the convoy. The driver pulled up alongside a wood, saying we would stay here for the rest of the night; but a commanding French officer spoke to the contrary. So once more we were on our way, sort of going it blind. This part of the journey extended through a deep forest with torn up roads, and this along with the black night made our journey more trying. We plowed on, however, and at daybreak caught up with the convoy. At 6 a.m. we unloaded the trucks and at once began to pitch tents in the woods. We knew we were drawing close to the lines, for artillery guns were sounding off frequently.

At 8:30 in the evening we packed up again, hiking to Saint-Jean-aux-Bois. Here we spent the day and learned of the big drive of the Allies. A big Allied offensive opened on the 16th with the 1st Division driving towards Soissons. All troops were concealed in woods so the numerous Boche planes hovering about were unaware of the imminent Allied offensive. At 7:30 p.m. we pulled up stakes again, moving toward the line of action to a point south of Soissons and Chateau-Thierry where the drive would start for us. After marching for an hour, a heavy rain set in and the night became black. Roads became so congested that the column of single file was broken time and time again, the rear losing its way. Tanks, cannons, supply trains, machine gun units, and infantry were all traversing this one road, which was torn up and muddy. With the drenching rain a more miserable night was never experienced up to this time. In a way this dark night was fortunate, for on a clear night Fritz would have slaughtered us with bombs.

Through this black and dismal outlook we plodded on, reaching the town of Montdidier at 2 a.m. Here we threw ourselves on the grass, awaiting orders to continue. At 3:30 a.m. we were up and going. While we marched along the roads, all our eyes were cast toward the lines, for we knew at 5 o'clock the signal calling for the artillery would go up to announce the attack was about to begin. Rockets of all descriptions were flying up everywhere along the line. Finally the actual earth quivered, as if to shake the very dome of the sky, when, at the sight of the continual signals for artillery, every cannon blazed away. From Belgium to the Swiss border, the cannons seemed to echo to our sector ... so great was the roar. We arrived at the jumping off place at 6:30 a.m. From our position as reserves, the infantry was seen mounting the hill in perfect skirmish order: first they disappeared from view; then they retreated back over the slope as a disorganized mass of humanity. With a blast of a whistle they immediately reformed their line, and back over the top they went. At 7:30 a.m. the advance was 4.5 kilometers, and still the artillery was blasting away a trail for the doughboys.

Trucks drew up near our position where thousands of more infantry continued on foot, waiting for the second wave to advance. Seven hundred prisoners were the first haul. These prisoners marched along, apparently much contented with their lot now. Many were but youngsters, 16 and 17 years old; others were old—all laughing and talking. The artillery began its movement forward as the advance at 10:30 a.m. was eight kilometers and still going. Thousands of prisoners were coming in with the first group waving and shaking hands with the next batch. A more contented lot you never saw. The War was over for them and presumably better living awaited them.

Now the scramble for souvenirs started. Many gas masks were taken from the prisoners before they reached the intelligence officer. At noon we got orders to push on and proceed to clean the debris from the roads. Villages were torn from their foundations, and houses were thrown across the road. Shell holes were plentiful. In the first village we approached, a wounded infantryman asked for aid and a cigarette. One of the men gave him attention, taking him to a first aid station. We now met hundreds of men requiring medical attention, most of whom were wounded in the arms and legs. Many Americans and Germans were seen lying in fields as part of the toll for the first day of the attack. All efforts were spent in clearing the way for the artillery advance. As we went on, the ghastly sights appeared before us. One doughboy was sitting in a shell hole, apparently resting; but on approaching nearer to him, he was found dead, held in the sitting position

Au Q. G. A., le 30 Juillet 1918

ORDRE GÉNÉRAL N° 318

Officiers, Sous-Officiers & Soldats, etc.

Epaule contre épaule avec vos camarades Français vous vous êtes jetés dans la bataille de contre-offensive qui a commencé le 18 juillet.

Vous y avez couru comme à une fête.

Votre élan magnifique a bousculé l'ennemi surpris et votre tenacité indomptable a arrêté le retour offensif de ses Divisions fraîches.

Vous vous êtes montrés les dignes Fils de votre Grand Pays et vous avez fait l'admiration de vos frères d'armes.

91 canons, 7.200 prisonniers, un butin immense, 10 kilomètres de terrain reconquis, voilà votre part dans les trophées de cette victoire.

En outre, vous avez acquis pleinement le sentiment de votre supériorité sur le barbare, ennemi du genre humain tout entier, contre lequel luttent les Enfants de la Liberté.

L'attaquer c'est le vaincre.

Camarades américains, je vous suis reconnaissant du sang généreusement versé sur le sol de ma Patrie.

Je suis fier de vous avoir commandé en de telles journées et d'avoir combattu avec vous pour la délivrance du monde.

Original text

A. H. Q., July 1918

GENERAL ORDER N° 318

Officers, N.C.O. & Men of the 3rd U.S.A.⋯

Shoulder to shoulder with your French Comrades, you hurled yourselves into the counter-offensive, which began July 18th.

You rushed to it as to a fête.

Your magnificent dash routed the unsuspecting enemy ⋯ your indomitable tenacity checked the offensive return his fresh Divisions.

You have shown yourselves to be worthy sons of your Gre⋯ Country and you have won the admiration of your Brothe⋯ in Arms.

91 cannon, 7.200 prisoners, an immence booty, 10 kilomet⋯ of reconquered ground, these are your trophies of victo⋯

Moreover, you have decisively demonstrated your superio⋯ over the barbarous enemy of the entire human ra⋯ against whom are struggling the Children of Liberty.

To attack him, is to vanquish him.

American Comrades, I am mindful of the blood which ⋯ have so generously spilled on the soil of my country.

I am proud to have commanded you throughout these d⋯ and to have fought with you for the Delivrance of the Wo⋯

Translation

Figure 13: General Order 318[92]

by the pack on his back. Farther on a German breathed his last breath, clutching the butt of his machine gun which was still on its tripod.

Coming to a ravine, two French soldiers were diligently guarding the entrance to two huge dugouts where two hundred prisoners were held awaiting their escort to the rear. Mounted on horses French lancers carrying the long spear were taking up their position ready to continue the advance in the morning. Tanks that were lined up along the edge of the gully were ready to creep up the hill and over at the signal. Here we halted and threw ourselves in a cabbage patch as the drone of Boche bombing planes hovered above us. The night was dark and there was no moon. Suddenly the whole area was lit up. More eagerly did we crouch low to the earth as the bombs poured down around us. There was neither shelter nor trenches—only the cold, dark earth on which to stretch out, and again the heavens were lit up bringing into view as it seemed every form of human being, animal, and wagon. Again the deadly bombs tore up the earth, shaking the ground as though an earthquake struck us. I glanced up and wondered whether there was a searchlight or perhaps a torch mounted on a sort of parachute. This was all I observed, for I was soon trying to dig my head into the dirt, because, for the third time, Fritz unloaded his bombs and went blasting away at some poor mortals.

We knew relief came, for we could now hear the dismal drone of the planes as they sank in the distance. At daybreak we were on the move. A short stretch along the road showed us part of the toll paid by the Boche bombing of the night before. A four-mule team and driver were completely wiped out: the mules were lying in the road; the driver was hurled twenty feet away and lay dead in the field. Further on houses gave evidence of being caught in the bombing. Soon we heard the roar of guns and the steady drive of the barrage, and we knew the Second Battle of the Marne was on for the second day. The country was practically void of any villages and lay open before us, and not until late in the afternoon did we come to a halt ... tired, hungry, and casting maledictions upon the Boche and every German alive.

We took positions in individual trenches across the Paris-Soissons road. This road no doubt was the most beautiful of all roads leading to the capital city but was now partially destroyed and obstructed by fallen trees. We kept these positions until Fritz, after wounding a few of our men when hurling missiles at our artillery along this road, drove us to the field in back. There I located in a ten-foot deep hole gouged out of the earth by a large German bomb. Two others occupied this hole with me, and we proceeded to adjust things and prepare for a bombing expedition by Fritz. From our hideout we had a good view of the French and American artillery guns which were hastily driven up by night team horses, rapidly put in place, and readied for action. With the open level country in the rear as a backdrop, it seemed as though the battle was being directed by a motion picture company—staging each gun as it was hurried up and twirled around; men loading, firing, and reloading again; quickly another gun being set in place and another and another till the whole battery was blazing away at the still retreating Boche.

We looked toward the lines and saw Germans coming over a hill; we seemed to think it was a counterattack while the guns shelled the hill. The guns soon changed their range as they discovered but ten Germans quickly marching towards us. No one stopped them so they kept coming till a company of engineers farther ahead took them prisoners. Our advance became so rapid now that many enemy machine gun nests went undiscovered by the infantry, but on passing these nests, the Germans unconcealed the nests and opened fire on our men in the rear. Many deaths resulted till the following wave of infantry battled the Germans and killed all. Tricks of this sort were plentiful with the Boche. Yet they feared death, which prompted them to place Red Cross[93] bands on their arms when about to be captured.

At dark we got orders to move forward, taking position behind the front lines between the infantry and artillery. It was the Germans' old front lines; and our entrance into these lines was hailed by a furious gas attack. It was no easy matter now to get situated in the dark while wearing gas masks. We picked our trenches the best we could, awaiting the morning. All during the night shells kept coming and going, and at intervals through the night gas alarms sounded. Three hours of sleep in the last three days was a great deal at this time, but the prospects of a long rest helped console us. At daybreak we got the first view of our surroundings. We were located on the slope of a hill facing the Germans, in front of a battery of artillery anchored along the Paris Highway. We knew here we would find hell, for no place is worse than being near artillery, which invites shellfire, bombs, and gas shells. The soldiers in the artillery sure do draw trouble to them, but they were giving it more than they were getting.

It was a constant rain of shells all night and day. The first day was about as uncomfortable a day and night as had been experienced. A shell coming over struck the top of a man's trench, burying both the man and the trench. Quick assistance soon unburied him, as he was completely covered with only his arm and hand exposed, waving it as though calling for help. Not long after this another bomb exploded near the edge of the road at the bottom of our hill and where two other fellows had their trench. This was too much for them, so with bag and baggage they moved to another hole.

From the hill on the other side of the road in front of us, a shell came rolling along; I ducked in my trench and gave it no more thought. Fifteen minutes later it was passed around that a shell hit, and one fellow was killed. I looked out and there was a lad lying on the ground four yards away directly opposite my trench with the top of his head off, while alongside lay the shell—the one I saw come rolling over the hill. This massive piece of steel tore away a path for itself in its mad rush along. A burying party was sent out that night and disposed of the body.

The shelling was coming from two directions all day, as we were in a sort of bowl, while at night the flash of the Boche guns was distinctly seen firing from the woods from their place of concealment. These shells were directed towards the artillery behind us but often fell short, scattering fragments of shells and dirt in our trenches. For five days and nights we were kept in our trenches, especially in the daytime. No one would dare come out, for Fritz could directly observe us since we were facing their lines, and a barrage laid along our hill would have annihilated the troops. Our meals consisted of the rations carried on our back, while at night we all would declare our heartfelt congratulations to our kitchen force who braved this heavy shellfire and bombs to bring one substantial feast with the warmth still lingering.

The third night I was ordered to take charge of the detail that was to take the pots and cans back to the wagons. This was an unpleasant task, and one that was not welcomed by any of the men. However, I rounded up enough men, and over the hill in the darkness we walked. The carrying party hurried ahead while I took up the rear. After dodging stakes and hurdling barbed wire, I stumbled across a huge carcass stretched on the ground. At first it appeared to be a horse without its legs. As my eyes became accustomed to the darkness, I realized that the carcass was that of a man. It was hard to believe that this huge massive form was that of a human being. No doubt he had fallen only a short time before we arrived; his body was puffed out almost to the bursting point. I could do nothing, so I hurried to catch up to my party.

We lost no time in disposing of the burden of the heavy pots, and we had but scarcely started our return journey when Fritz let fly a shower of bombs behind us. All lay down till Fritz was through, then I signaled all to proceed. Thinking all were safe we marched back to our trenches. I checked up and found one man missing. I felt responsible, so before reporting him as missing, I waited. In twenty minutes back he came, and I tell you, after his tale, I did not believe so much could happen in twenty minutes.

He failed to hear us signal to return. Trying to get back, he lost his way. He passed along the road in front of our hill and reached a gully just as Fritz commenced shelling. He dove into a shell hole which he found was occupied when he landed on top of a form. Because he was crouching low as Fritz was shelling hard now, he paid no attention to the form. Later on he discovered the form was a dead body. He and the dead man kept company till Fritz subsided. Then he started hunting for home. As Fritz had him jumping from shell hole to shell hole, he soon jumped into his own trench. Well soon Fritz was back again flying very low with his aeroplane loaded with bombs, all of which he dumped along the Paris road. That trip was his last one for the night.

We welcomed the morning for we were badly in need of something to smoke to soothe our nerves. Fortunately the sun was out bright, as the only means of lighting our pipes or cigarettes was with a magnifying glass. We had no matches. I looked out toward the road where three men were walking. A shell exploded behind them, killing one instantly. Up the road a distance were two wagons, one behind the other, each being pulled at a fair clip by four mules. Shells were exploding along the road following the wagons. One wagon stopped after the lead pair of mules was killed. The driver got up and off, unhitched the dead pair of mules and, with shells exploding around, dashed off in the wagon driven by the two remaining mules. It was a critical moment, but the calmness and direct movements were surprising in itself and interesting to watch.

For the fourth day we all kept to our trenches under Fritz's canopy of shellfire. Boche planes flying low were out in great numbers, and, when they flew over the trenches, they fired at us with machine guns. For fifteen minutes we were dead a hundred times with Fritz and Company peppering away. So low did they fly that many fellows got their rifles in action hoping to bring one of those invaders down. Night brought no relief for the bombers were out for vengeance.

The fifth day dawned with word that a detachment from Scotland was to relieve us at night. At noon an advance party of Scots came looking over our home, but they explained that they would not be staying here ... that just as soon as Gerry[94] (as they called the Germans) knew anyone was here, he would tear up the hill. One Scotchman sat on the parapet of my trench, and in reply to my telling him to climb down into the trench as Fritz was sending shells over, he said, "No, if I get a blighty,[95] I'll go home, and if he kills me, I'll never know it." He said with four years of this grind and no end to the war, it made no difference how soon the end came for him. He went on to say that just last night after hiking from Ypres, thirty men were killed or wounded by a bomber who observed the light from cigarettes during their rest on the march. Although we Americans had strict orders regarding lights at night, these fellows coolly ignored any such caution. I listened to the Scotchman tell of how they had planned their gas attack on the Germans to drive them out of concrete dugouts in the Ypres sector and how all was arranged to send a cloud of gas over the line of fire. The night of the attack the wind changed, blowing towards them, so the attack failed. However, one massive charge by the Scots captured the trenches and dugouts.

That noon we heard the Boche coming, blowing the ground up at a lively rate. The Boche seemed to think a relief was taking place so sent a barrage over to advance the attack. As we were directly behind the infantry, we felt the time for action had come. Orders were hastened to load and fix bayonets. Here for the first time I bade good-bye to my notes on this diary, burying this book alongside my trench, fearing its capture by the Germans in case of a successful attack by them. The Americans immediately counterattacked, driving the Germans to their own line of trenches. I saw nothing coming over the hills, so I judged that our artillery and doughboys had stopped their advance. Nearing nightfall this Scottish detachment left us, and nothing more was heard from them until midnight. At midnight we heard bagpipes blowing at a great rate, and as we filed out, the Scots known as the Gordon Highlanders,[96] led by their bagpipes band, marched in. They were sure welcome to our abode.

We hiked six kilometers and camped in a woods for that whole day and night. We awaited the arrival of trucks to take us back for a long period of rest. At ten o'clock we boarded the trucks, arriving at Beaumarchais 7 o'clock that night. In a few days the whole Division was assembled in this area. The Signal Corps[97] that camped here with us had a thirteen-year-old Belgium boy as a mascot. This lad was four years in the trenches with the French Blue Devils. He was a great worker and was happy dressed in an American uniform. He was learning English rapidly and caught on to the slang words with no trouble at all. His parents were killed in the invasion of Belgium by the Germans. He escaped while visiting friends in another part of Belgium, having time to flee before the Boche arrived. Upon our departure he was turned over to the authorities much to his regret and that of the men in the Signal Corps, for the lad made good use of himself by peeling spuds and cleaning kitchen utensils. [Ed. Charles Edward Dilkes noted General Orders 9, 38, and 143 and a tribute from Major General Reed, which are included in the Appendix: 153+. Soldiers of the First Division were awarded the Victory Medal for their participation in the Aisne-Marne Campaign, Appendix: 157.]

THE WAR DIARY IN PICTURES

Washington, D.C., to St. Nazaire
Charles Edward Dilkes in 1st Engineers - Co F (back row: fifth from right)
Unknown - Dilkes Family Collection

St. Nazaire to Lunéville
40 hommes—8 chevaux
"Going to the front"
George Myers

Storming of Cantigny
Messenger bi-plane "Dutch [Deutch] aero coming out of the clouds"
George Myers

Storming of Cantigny
Casualties after
German gas attack
"Chepy - all gases used"
George Myers

Storming of Cantigny
Carrier Pigeon for communications "Cantigny messenger"
George Myers

Aisne-Marne Campaign
Soissons
"400 prisoners in caves hid by cavalry"
George Myers

Aisne-Marne
Campaign

Soissons

"Engineers
camouflage
trenches"

George Myers

Aisne-Marne
Campaign

Battle of
Château-Thierry

"Hill 204"

George Myers

St. Mihiel Drive
Delousing clothes in
a boiler
"Cooties"
George Myers

St. Mihiel Drive
Town liberated by
Americans
"Nonsard - St. Mihiel"
George Myers

St. Mihiel Drive

Demolished
dwellings in
Apremont

"Apremont"

George Myers

Meuse-Argonne
Operation

American camp
on site of Battle
of Verdun

"Camp Hill 304"

*Unknown - Dilkes
Family Collection*

Meuse-Argonne
Operation
American camp
"Argonne"
George Myers

Meuse-Argonne
Operation
Dead German
soldiers
"Argonne field"
*Unknown - Dilkes
Family Collection*

Meuse-Argonne
Operation

Captured
German
prisoners

"Prisoners—
Argonne"

George Myers

Sedan

"Captured
ammunition
dump train"

George Myers

TOUL-SAIZERAIS SECTOR

On July 28th I was sent with a detail to Ormoy-villers to load artillery equipment and the mule wagons onto trains preparatory to the Division moving towards Toul. We arrived at Toul on July 31st at 6:30 a.m. From here we hiked eight kilos to Blenod-les-Toul where for three days we rested up and were given the opportunity for forty-eight hour passes. As these passes entitled us to visit a town where there was nothing but a few village huts, three of us boarded the Paris express for Troyes. The train was crowded, and hence we were forced to stand up through the whole journey; we could not move either way for fear of tramping on someone sleeping in the narrow passage way.

At daybreak we reached Troyes where we became cautious less we meet any of the military police. The French guards allowed us to pass unchallenged, and soon we arrived at a hotel, engaging rooms for the night. Later we learned it was the officers' hotel, so this made us still more careful. After resting up for awhile, another lad and I set out to explore the town, and we had gotten well advanced into the city proper when we observed an MP[98] walking toward us. We turned the first corner to avoid him when we marched right into the arms of another.

I jumped into a vegetable store where I thought I was not seen, bought some tomatoes, and commenced to juggle them. As the MP did not come in, I looked out and there I saw him talking to my companion. I told the woman shopkeeper why I was lingering. Then I saw the crowd in the store look outside, and they, seeing the MP and watching me juggling the tomatoes, set up a howl.

Because the argument was getting hotter outside, I thought it time I made my appearance. The lad was telling the police that if they put him on a train, he would only hop another and come back. Finally we appealed to his sense of good fellowship, so with a warning to keep undercover, he let us go.

Fortunately we met with no other military police although we were out the whole day. Hence, the first pass since my arrival in France was a hummer[99] in every respect. We reached our camp the next day and found everyone hustling to get ready for departure. At noon on August 5th trucks convoyed us to Rosieres. Then we hiked to Puvenelle and on to the Pont-a-Mousson Sector to our camp in the woods where we were billeted in shacks.

We were ushered in by a heavy rainstorm, falling into ditches, brush, and mud, as the walk through the dense woods with no lights took a bit of skillful maneuvering. Our sojourn here was a schooling in building defensive positions, fortifying trenches, constructing effective positions for machine gun fire, and laying barbed wire. On August 7th I was sent to the second line trenches to sketch these various strong points. I noted the well-constructed line of man trenches and communicating trenches and the careful design of the concrete dugouts. This was a sector principally for such schooling, but at times when Fritz became aware of any working parties, he sent his salute over which made things mighty uncomfortable in this area. Bombing expeditions were carried out frequently, and each night as we lay in our flimsy structure of a barrack, the feeling of complete annihilation seemed imminent.

During the day the shrapnel from the anti-aircraft guns and many duds would find their way to our quarters with many of the pieces battering at the roof of our abode. It was ducking here, there, and everywhere while it was chancy with the duds. A greater number of these duds would fall about our shack, but remarkable to state, none hit it.

The dread of the Boche planes at night was felt more here for the reason that there was no protection, and these large shacks offered a likely target for Fritz's shells. The explosion of a shell, or the sound of a siren to warn of an approaching shell, made a ghastly noise echoing through the woods.

On August 12th I was sent out in charge of a detail of doughboys putting up barbed wire when Fritz threw six shells in succession at our point of working—one striking a hard rock, sending the fragments in all directions. Only the throwing of ourselves quickly to the ground saved many injuries.

Much propaganda was sent over the lines. At one time the French would tie reading matter to a balloon and let it sail ahead with the wind. Then another time a balloon would come sailing in our direction but drift too far behind our lines for us to go after the pamphlets. The French had many of these notes, some asking for tobacco or stating to come over and give up, and such other pieces of propaganda.

We spent much time in talking over our last battle at Soissons with the infantry. A lad working in my detail related how every officer and non-commissioned officer of his battalion was killed or wounded, and when Fritz came over in a raid, the privates took command of the battalion and made a countermove. The spirit of the infantry at all times was highly commendable. On the third day of the attack at Soissons, a man riding a horse dashed up to the infantry commander, stating he had orders from General Foch[100] to retreat to a certain point. He was dealt with accordingly when it was soon learned he was a spy and attempted to hold up the advance.

Fritz woke us up on the morning of the 17th with a terrific barrage and a raid. This raid was checked by our infantry who followed it up with their raid. It was then our infantry discovered items hanging on the barbed wire in front of the Boche trenches: tin cans, bells, and grenades that would signal the approach of anyone entering their wired area. The distance between front lines was considerable at this point and was made so by mutual agreement, for at the beginning of the War the lines were but a few yards apart. Many deaths occurred by the throwing of hand grenades over and into each other's trenches, so when each side drew back, neither knew how far the other was going. Thus the distance became great and remained so.

THE U.S. ARMY TAKES COMMAND

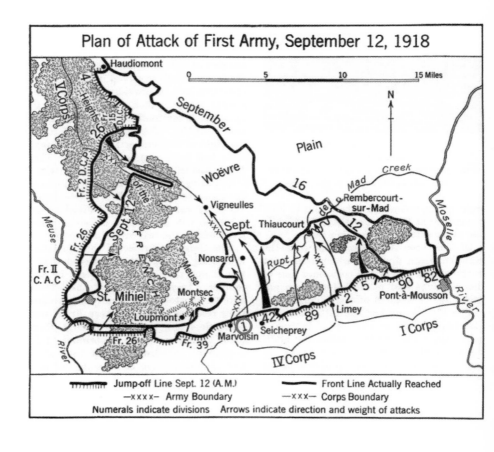

Figure 14: Map of St. Mihiel: Plan of Attack[101]

VIII

ST. MIHIEL DRIVE

The French had many peaceful days in Soissons and complained of the Americans now demoralizing conditions with their incessant firing. On August 22nd we took our first delousing[102] when all clothes were thrown in a huge boiler and steamed out. We were free of cooties[103] for an hour or so anyway, and this was a big relief. At twelve o'clock that night we were ordered to move, and so we hiked to Rosieres. We left Rosieres at 7:30 a.m., hiking twenty-six kilos to Blenod-les-Toul, arriving at three o'clock p.m. On August 24th we again set out, leaving in trucks for Gerauvillers where we made our camp for a few days.

Our stay at Gerauvillers was short but restful. Infantry drills and engineer drills were the program outlined by the officers, while the men outlined plans for card playing and carousels with *vin blanc* and *vindy rouge*. At evening a stampede followed the arrival of the newspapers. As the paper showed the battle line each day, it was with much interest we saw its gradual drawing back towards Germany. Since the opening of the big offensive on July 18th, there had been no lull, but more vigorous was the battle being waged. Drilling was the order for each day till on the 30th the whole Division was called to Vaucouleurs for maneuvers.

On Friday, August 30th, the Division was assembled in a wide stretch of country just to the east of Vaucouleurs. Here the maneuvers were carried out as though a battle was being staged. The infantry formed their skirmish lines of first, second, and third waves; the engineers assembled wire cutting squads, while bangalore[104] squads were grouped in small detachments with the various companies of infantry. The artillery took their position in the rear, making ready to send their usual deadly barrage. With everything ready, we set out over the hills, capturing towns and winding up at our objective at three o'clock in the afternoon. While walking beside an infantryman, I remarked that this territory is quite similar to Montsec. He agreed with me, but we had no idea these maneuvers were in preparation to attack Montsec and that the impregnable Montsec would be taken by us.

At five o'clock we were back in camp, cleaning up equipment for the usual inspection on Saturday. Outside of inspection, Saturday was a day we all welcomed because it was the one day we could do pretty much as we pleased, provided one did not get caught. However, our town went dry of wine, so another fellow and I tried the neighboring village called Badonvilliers about two kilometers away. It was like a regular United States country town: a population of about fifty people, twenty-five horses with customary manure piles, a couple of stores, and many cafés. Here we felt as if we were in a typical American country pool room with its big stove and bare walls and the usual swapping of lies.

By the time four o'clock came we decided on a plan to rent a couple of bicycles and ride to Vaucouleurs. We felt ready for most anything now, so we got the bikes and away we went. Our start was at the top of a hill which extended to a gradual slope for the three-kilometer ride to Vaucouleurs. All there was to do was to sit and coast at a good pace for these three kilometers, and then we pushed up a hill and coasted down another, and so on. About six o'clock we arrived at Vaucouleurs, got the fellow in charge of the storeroom there to take care of our bikes, and then we set out for a real honest meal. About eight o'clock we started to take in the sights. We soon learned that we were not popular in this town for up to nine o'clock we were still walking by ourselves, and now the streets were beginning to thin out somewhat with the various stores closing. We thought it best if we got undercover before an MP put us undercover. We had just finished talking about this when one MP stepped up to me and in a gruff tone said, "Do you belong here?" I answered, "Yes." "That's good," he said. "What outfit?" he asked. I answered, "Headquarters." Then he seemed satisfied and off we went. We managed to make a bed for ourselves in the storeroom. It was not the most comfortable bed, for it was the stone floor to the shack. Taking some blankets, canvas covers, etc., we put in enough hours of sleep before daybreak, and then we set out for home. The few MPs we passed on leaving the town let us go, evidently thinking we were a couple of jokes on bicycles up early in the morning. We returned the bikes without a puncture. Then we set out over the hills for home.

On Monday, September 2nd, we left at two o'clock in the morning, hiking twenty-three kilometers to Void, arriving at 7:30 a.m. We left at seven o'clock p.m., September 3rd, arriving at Jouy-sous-les-Côtes at eleven o'clock. This was our second trip to Jouy-sous-les-Côtes, but now the inhabitants seemed very much thinned out. Perhaps they had left, owing to the intended massing of troops around this sector and inevitable consequences from the presence of so many troops. However, for myself, I had one long picnic during my stay here, although I failed to comprehend the gayety of it all and the reason for such merriment. One old man, who we got in tow, could buy the choicest wine, which helped to make merry our sojourn. An hour or so of each day was devoted to instructions in handling bangalores: assembling the bangalore tubes, charging them, and discharging a few as an experiment.

I took a walk up to the huge fort overlooking Montsec, viewing no-man's-land for the third time. I saw the system of trenches and fortifications of the Boche, and although nothing definite was given out that an attack was to be made here, we all had a strong presentiment that such was the plans. I was just beginning now to realize, as I looked over the hills towards the Boche lines, what a colossal affair an enterprise, such as was being planned behind our lines, was going to be. I pondered what a tremendous loss of life, what a slaughter will necessarily follow the taking of that impregnable position of Montsec, and what an obstruction and death trap those impenetrable forests to the right, left, and beyond would be.

I knew from our previous stay at this sector what a vast amount of artillery was placed in the forests on those hills; and now we were to attempt what the French with the loss of forty thousand men failed to do. It was very gratifying at this time to see a priest in the village—an American who heard confessions and administered communion to all who wished to avail themselves of probably the last rights to be administered to them. Gradually it began to dawn upon us the magnitude of the conflict that was to be waged. In our leisure moments we heard of the persistent driving of the Allies from Ypres to Reims, forcing the Boche back kilometer after kilometer. I was talking to one of the French Blue Devils who just came

Living History

[LESSONS LEARNED FROM THE ST. MIHIEL OPERATION]
ORGANIZATION OF MEUSE-ARGONNE OPERATION

First Army, A. E. F.,

Office of the Chief of Staff,

P. C. Ligny-en-Barrois,

September 17, 1918.

FROM: Chief of Staff

TO: Commanding General,

      I Corps, A. E. F.; III Corps, A. E. F.; V Corps, A. E. F.

[Extract]

The army commander desires you be informed of the following:

General Plan: As indicated in the plan submitted [Sept. 16, 1918] to corps commanders, the First Army in conjunction with Allied Armies, will execute an attack between the Meuse and the Argonne.

*****

Corps commanders are advised that the divisions in their new commands were not engaged in the St-Mihiel operation and therefore have not had that experience. There were many lessons gained in said operation especially in relation to passage of wire, the employment of tanks in liaison with the infantry, and the circulation on the roads. These lessons should be brought to the attention of the divisions. **The large-handled wire cutters used with such success in the St-Mihiel operation will be sent at once to depots in the French Second Army. Special steps should be taken to have these reach divisions.**[105]

By command of General Pershing:

H. A. DRUM, Colonel, Chief of Staff.

United States Army Center of Military History (1998), "Military Operations of the American Expeditionary Forces," *United States Army in World War I,* version 2, CD-ROM disc 1 of 3, volume IX: 79.

from Soissons. He said the Americans were fighting hard, but going too fast. They captured German guns and made the German prisoners destroy their own guns.

On September 8th I was chosen for guard duty. About ten o'clock at night troops began passing through the town—not hundreds, but thousands. Artillery pieces of all descriptions passed by, including guns that were so big that a man could crawl into them. Tanks in great numbers were ushered in and out, making for their respective locations behind the line of attack. These indications were the first that a great battle was close at hand. Contrary to the usual routine of guard duty, I was not relieved after twenty-four hours on duty. I was to do guard duty all day up to twelve o'clock that night when orders for leaving camp came and with them the release of all those in custody. We left camp at 2:00 a.m. during the dark hours of the early morning and hiked to our station in the woods behind Raulecourt, arriving there at five o'clock. The congestion of troops and wagons was more dense than at Soissons. Many men fell asleep on their feet, toppling over only to be run over by some wagon.

We rested that day, and at night details were sent out to begin cutting paths through our barbed wire. In the morning we awoke to find things beginning to happen. Breakfast? Well, we had been over a year in France, but never did we feast on such a breakfast as this. We had steak, potatoes with butter, and coffee—you could not believe it. We had become accustomed to getting one or two slices of bread, and now we had all we wanted. Of course this was better than telling us that this breakfast was to be the last breakfast we would ever have, so they were giving us the best. After breakfast the details were posted. We noted our places and also the places of those that were left behind. This caused no wonder because we knew, although we were not told, that those men held behind were to train the new recruits after the battle.

Things were beginning to get more exciting, and all seemed to be in high spirits. The tanks commenced assembling; the roads and woods were littered with them. Cannons, large and small, and troops by the thousands were here, there, and everywhere, waiting nightfall to take their positions at the lines. At eleven o'clock eight men and I were assigned as wire cutters to the 26th Infantry, Company E, 2nd Platoon and proceeded to the camp of the 26th Infantry. We received our orders and then waited for the time to move forward. At six o'clock the avalanche began rolling ahead through a torrent of rain, mud, and congested roads and fields, but with little noise and confusion.

We reached the crossroads outside Mandres, which were under considerable shelling. We were delayed there for two hours, standing rain-soaked, and waiting for the guide to conduct us to our position in the trenches. We were glad to get moving again although this time it was through knee-deep muddy trenches. We plowed through these trenches in quick time for we were considerably late. We were still wading through one trench or going over the top into another trench when, as though at a single blast, the heavens lit up as the thousands of cannons belched forth fire and steel in the awakening of the first all-American attack. At one o'clock this timely bombardment set forth with all its ravenous hate the vengeance stored up for many months, and now with exceptional pressure hammered at the gates of freedom. While scurrying through the trenches, blazing away at unseen targets far beyond, I saw that Montsec had become a lone target for hundreds of guns. Fire would belch forth from its peak, as the huge shells exploded there, just like a volcano.

At two o'clock we were still wending our way through this trench and then another, and still the cannons thundered and roared, blazing away at all possible obstructions. At three o'clock there was no abatement, but with increasing fury were these missiles hurled at the enemies' fortifications. At four o'clock we thought of nothing but opening a free path all the way to the outlying fortifications around Metz. We had now gained our positions in the trenches and, leaning against the muddy walls of the trenches, we awaited the orders to go over. Soon word passed along to load and fix bayonets. Just then I jammed my gun into the dirt in taking it from my shoulder. In trying to get the mud from the barrel I jammed it worse. My gun was no good to me now, that was sure, but I knew it would not be long after the attack started that I would have another, if I still lived.

At 4:30 a.m. the order came for engineers over the top. Immediately we began hacking away at the barbed wire clearing four paths. How many shells exploded around us I do not know, for the excitement and roar of our own guns left us unconscious to any approach of hostile shells or explosions. We now took our position in squad column[106] with the infantry ready to advance when the barrage for attack opened up. At five o'clock

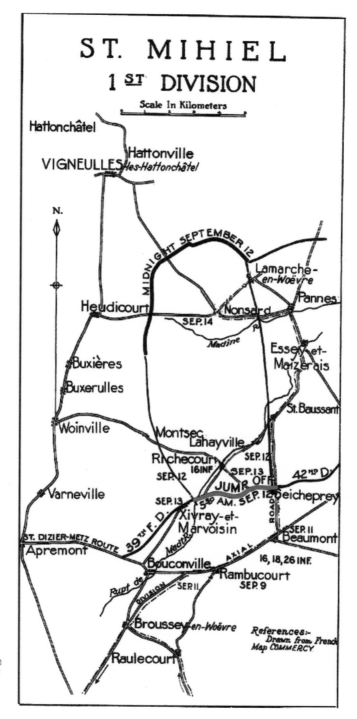

Figure 15:
Map of
St. Mihiel:
1st Division
Positions[107]

hell broke loose with the first wave sweeping toward the German front lines. Shells began to break in our midst but did no damage. A little resistance was met by the first wave from machine gun fire but was overcome, and the advance went on. The first wave had gained its objective. At seven o'clock the second wave leapfrogged the first wave. We pressed on when at about 9:30 our second wave, pushing along with the first wave, got ahead of the barrage.

Shells began to explode around us, fired from our own guns; but soon the shelling ceased. Onward we rushed, now and then holding when the right or left was held up due to machine gun fire. On our left the delay was now considerable as the Boche from a church steeple were using effective fire from one-pound guns and machine guns. A tank drew up to the town and soon brought six Germans down. Germans were coming over the hills in groups now only too eager to give themselves up. At a period of rest we took to a trench, and soon four Germans came running around crying, "*Kamerad.*" They presented us with souvenirs, including the eagerly sought after Iron Cross,[108] even though they hated to part with them. One reluctantly handed me his Iron Cross and asked for water. I wanted to give him some, but the whistle to start ahead sounded, so we sent them to the rear and pushed onward.

The wave in front had not gained its objective. We now assumed the skirmish line, leapfrogged this wave, and pushed forward with no one in front but the enemy. We had gone but a short distance when an enemy machine gun began sweeping about in front of us. The order came for all hands to get down, and as the bullets whizzed over our heads, we endeavored to bore ourselves into the earth. How far over our heads they were going we did not know, but the sound was mighty uncomfortable. In a few minutes a machine gun barrage was opened up by our machine gunners. Then complete silence followed; shortly thereafter, the whistle sounded to advance. It was all done quickly and orderly. The enemy was located and fought to the last. One enemy soldier was concealed under the ground, having a thin covering of earth and the rest of the ground as camouflage, with the barrel of his gun protruding out from this covering. He had hoped to delay the advance.

A little farther on we ran into crossfire with shells exploding on a knoll directly in front of us and seeming to careen off this knoll, passing through our lines and exploding again in the rear. Here we had to stay close to the ground, but how no one was killed from those shells is still a puzzle to me. As each shell passed over us, I glanced back to see that the mass of troops coming up from the rear was lying as close to the ground as they could. The enemy machine gun was soon quieted by the troops farther advanced to our left. Again the order to proceed sounded. In looking around over the wide expanse of territory unobstructed, troops were coming over the hills for as far as the eye could see.

To my left and right the steady marching of men formed an endless chain. We had reached the top of a hill when in the valley below shrapnel, high explosives, and golden rain threatened any trespassing. Down the hill we went straight for the valley with its death dealing devices. I thought now that this moment was my last, for lead and fire were raining in there; and still we went on. Just as we neared the bottom, the shelling ceased, and with it a deep sigh from all in my vicinity.

At three o'clock we had gained the final objective of the day. Immediately we dug in, going into a captured town near by, helping ourselves to straw and covering, which the Germans left in their hasty retreat. We returned to our trench only to receive orders to take up the pursuit immediately to capture a railroad train ahead. Just before nightfall we made entry into a deep forest. Through these thick woods we walked till eleven o'clock at night, and then, assured that we were lost with little prospect of finding the railroad, orders came to halt and make the best of things for the night. We all sank to the ground where we halted and soon fell asleep. Later on officers approached with flashlights endeavoring to locate our position.

At daybreak we were on the move, and in half an hour we crossed the tracks of the railroad, which the night before seemed impossible to find. We followed this railroad that stretched through this deep forest for five kilometers, and we saw that the forest concealed vast stores of supplies, engines, equipment, huts, and canteens. The railroad was in good condition, also the stations, but the canteens and huts were demolished by fire. At 12:30 p.m. the chug of a locomotive with our prey aboard was distinctly heard. The locomotive escaped us, but later we learned of its capture along with 1,500 Germans trying to make their escape.

Shelling was heard close by, but we knew it was not from our artillery as we had gone too fast; and no time was given them to haul their cannons up with the rapid advance. A shell had put a halt to a wagonload of food and equipment, scattering its contents over the road. The wagonload evidently was ransacked by troops ahead of us. The four years of occupation by the Germans of this territory had all the usual German signs about stations and roads, such as "*Rauchen Verboten*" (Smoking Forbidden), and also signs indicating directions to towns now called by German names.

At four o'clock we halted and began digging in for the night. Unexpectedly we were called from the lines at five o'clock, and while back on the road awaiting the assembly of all the engineer units, hot coffee and small cakes were given to us prepared by the German prisoners with their captured kitchen. These Germans were also busy slaughtering and making ready a huge pig as supper for the infantry. At six o'clock we were on our long march back to a battered-down town where we camped for the night.

On September 14th we arrived at Apremont where nothing remained but a few walls of demolished dwellings. At one end of the town was a steep hill thickly populated with trees and brush. Here we found well-established quarters once occupied by the Boche. There were huts of all descriptions, each having a stove, cooking utensils, and a piano. Another shack was used as a canteen and recreation room. Here we helped ourselves to a piano, carrying it to a shack now occupied by our men. This piano helped along the amusement during our stay. A garden close by furnished fresh vegetables for supper that night, and a real elaborate meal was prepared. This meal was certainly welcomed after three days of corned beef and hard-tack.[109] At night we were entertained with German bombs, but none were close enough to cause uneasiness.

The next morning men were sent around to explode all articles that were lying around, seeming to be souvenirs, and looking suspicious. Many of these articles were found with wire attached but were set off before any souvenir hunters came to pick them up. The place was littered with infernal machines of all descriptions. The Company was immediately sent on roadwork, repairing and filling in the deep craters and reconstructing roads in general, as many of these roads had not been touched to any extent for four years and no doubt were seldom used since they were battered by shellfire. On the 20th the Division left the lines with the large city of Metz but twelve kilometers away. We boarded trains at seven o'clock at Gironville, arriving at four o'clock the next morning at Seraucourt in the Verdun sector. At 10:30 we hiked twenty kilometers toward the lines, camping in a French camp that night. [Ed. Charles Edward Dilkes noted General Orders 6, 56, and 238 and tributes from President Woodrow Wilson, British General Haig, and General Foch on the successful drive for St. Mihiel, which are included in the Appendix: 158+. Soldiers of the First Division were awarded the Victory Medal for their participation in the St. Mihiel Campaign, Appendix: 162.]

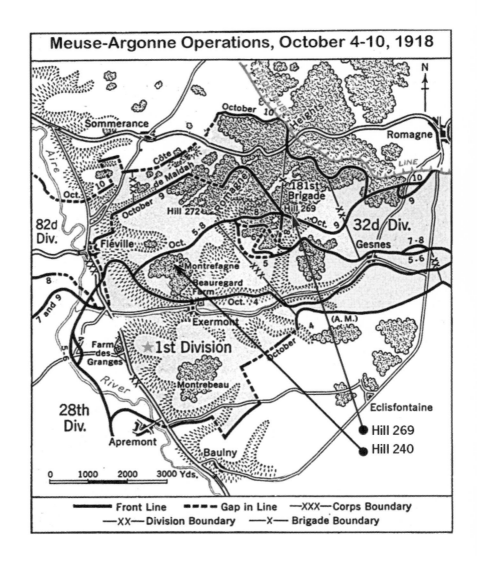

Figure 16: Map of the Meuse-Argonne Campaign: Phase 2[110]

MEUSE-ARGONNE OPERATION

On September 28th, the Division was off again on a twenty-kilometer march, and we knew it was not to a rest camp. Continuously the Division had been on the march and in the lines, allowing but enough time to strengthen the various units up to war measure. The companies with their full quota of men were now wending their way to another battlefield accompanied by heavy rain, while the torn up roads and muddy surface made this nightly march just as miserable as the others. Report had it that trucks were to convoy us; yet mile after mile we walked, and no trucks were in sight.

After we felt we had no more energy to walk any further, the order came to halt and make ready for camp. Everyone was so fatigued that no time was taken to pitch tents. Although the heavy rains were still beating down, we just threw our blankets over us, avoided the mud puddles, and found sleep in this manner most enjoyable.

At daybreak we all went about making fires to dry our rain-soaked clothes and thaw out a bit. We were able to get an idea of our location as soon as the sun peeped over the monstrous hills of Verdun. For the first time we had pitched camp in no-man's-land among these hills. The trenches were considerably torn away, while a few stakes remained which at one time held the wire entanglements. The roads, which were to receive our attention, were impassable, so their repair became the daily work of the troops till a passageway was made for the artillery and supply trains. The repairing of these roads was most urgent at this time for the battle was not to cease—for the drive to Berlin was critical.

On October 2nd hurried orders to shoulder the rifle and backpack once more drew us from our work. After fifteen miles of marching, the Division camped in a field south of the Argonne Forest. Our arrival was ushered in by a fusillade of shots and shells that drove our Headquarters' Company, which was taking up positions, helter-skelter in a sort of ravine. Shells broke in their midst, killing and wounding both mules and men. All became confused by this sudden attack; yet it was expected, for the enemy's observation balloons could be distinctly seen, and certainly our movements were observed by them.

We did not relish our position here, and while pitching tents, a feeling of uneasiness prevailed. Again we had two observation balloons directly behind us while artillery was blazing away at some unknown targets. Just as I expected, Fritz was coming over with his aeroplanes, which were flying at a low altitude ... so low in fact that our machine guns, rifles, and anti-aircraft guns were hurling their missiles, endeavoring to bring one down. This was my first shot at the enemy and a good miss at that.

Fritz did not come over by ones or twos, but in droves. As we watched this audacity, we became immediately interested in planes swooping down upon the Boche, coming from the direction of the dense forest to our right. All planes were now considerably lower than any we had seen. Our firing from machine guns and rifles ceased, but we still heard the rat-a-tat sound from the aeroplane guns pounding away. Suddenly one Boche was seen doing the loop-the-loop to the ground, falling but 200 yards from us. The American flyer who brought him down was seen to gradually come down himself. In a few minutes the American flyer was brought over to our camp where he said that he had brought down his first German aeroplane; however, in his eagerness to view his prey and make sure of his prize, he came too low to the ground, demolishing his plane in barbed wire set up near our camp. Things quieted down after this, while in the distance the Boche were seen wending their way over their lines.

We found ourselves at a crossroad with long-range artillery alongside of us. We realized this position held nothing but misfortune for us all. We were not disturbed by enemy shells, but clearly our position was known by the numerous enemy planes hovering overhead and flying low. Friday, October 4th, found us working on the shell-torn roads in Very. This town was once, but now is no more. All houses were completely demolished;

however, the remaining walls afforded a likely shield for our artillery that was in abundance throughout the town.

We had not been working long when Fritz drew us all under shelter by a continuous barrage of gas shells, necessitating the wearing of gas masks at various periods. From our work here one witnessed the most ghastly sights as the wounded infantry were escorted through the town, bringing tales of terrific slaughter. These units were of other divisions, but we knew our turn was coming. A war correspondent, Lt. Col. Frederick Palmer,[111] wrote an account of what happened next:

"The First was given the place of honor in the general attack of October 4th, and a place of honor in the Argonne battle was to be costly though glorious.

"Since my return home I have been asked if Belleau Woods was our most brilliant action. One answers: Brilliant in what respect? In battle efficiency? In courage? For at the front we thought of divisions only in the terms of efficiency.... I should place in even higher esteem than Belleau Woods the drive of the 1st and 2nd Divisions toward Soissons in July and possibly still higher that drive which the 1st was now to make. We had a dozen Belleau Woods in the Argonne.

"The First was a Regular Division, the pioneer of our Divisions in France, the longest trained, but it was not regular in the old sense, being better than regular in my mind, as we have understood the word regular in the past. Many of its young officers were out of the training camps, and the men who had filled the gaps in the ranks had come from the volunteers or the draft in all parts of the country. It was amazing how soon that divisional machine made a recruit a regular.

"I think that possibly when the First Division went into the Argonne battle it was the most efficient American Division that ever wore shoe leather. And Summerall in Command. He had led the First in the drive toward Soissons. He is a leader compounded of all kinds of fighting qualities, a crusader, and a calculating tactician, who, some say, can be as gentle as the sweetest natured chaplain, while others say, that he is nothing but brimstone and ruthless determination. The First with Summerall in command. We knew it would go through. It had always gone through. This was the part cast for the First in the A.E.F. We knew it would not attack in too great density, for that is not being mean and nasty to your enemy. Its battalion commanders would not hesitate in an emergency, and its veteran gunners would roll barrages of fire accurately and steadily in front of the infantry. Where strong points resisted, the artillery would be prompt with its blast of destruction to clear the way. 'As per schedule' begins the account of this operation—the coldest prose I have ever read for as hot a piece of work as I have ever seen.

"The Germans had a hot reception for the First, but the First expected this. It was due on those heights unless the Germans forgot the art of war. Four new divisions were identified on the First's front on the first day's attack.

"Constantly, undaunted by casualties, the Division kept plowing ahead, blasting the enemy's counterattacks before he could bring enough troops to bear, keeping the initiative in its own hands. There were delays from scorching machine gun fire down the roads and ravines, on the slopes of Hill 240, from gas and shell as well as machine gun fire, delays before machine gun fastnesses that would have baffled inexperienced hands, but no prolonged repulses.

"For eight days altogether the First was fighting steadily, not taking bites but in determined persistent action.... When the First came out, its losses were over 9,000 killed and wounded. Half of its infantry was out of action. It had paid the price, but it was the price of a vital success ... not only the First but the other divisions which fought through the machine gun nests and underbrush were capable of deeds which make Lookout Mountain appear somewhat less of a battle by comparison than some of us think it was. The First had relieved the pressure on the 77th Division thus helping to extricate the 'Lost Battalion,' and opened the door, closed by crossfire, for the 28th Division, somewhat beleaguered, but now pressing forward on the other side of the Aire Valley at the forest's edge, to repay the First in kind by helping to relieve it of fire from across the valley...."

CFDAEF: 10[112]

On October 5th we found that the second day of the attack through the Argonne met with the same stubborn resistance. As the day previous, we received orders to move up farther, where we camped along the side of a hill leading to a deep valley beneath.

In the valley an artillery unit with all its animals, equipment, and tents were massed, which to me seemed to invite disaster. From my hole along

Figure 17: Map of the Meuse-Argonne Campaign: Oct. 7-10[113]

the slope, I could only hope that Fritz would not become aware of this camp below. However it came. Fritz stirred things up and soon cleared every man from the valley, and only those manning the guns remained to return a few of the shells now pouring into the area. Horses, men, and wagons were blown up while the Boche overhead supported the encounter with bombs.

I watched a German aeroplane flying overhead and soon saw the wigwagging of a bomb leave the plane. The pilot was flying rather low, and from my position it looked as though the bomb was labeled for me. I crouched low just as it exploded: two horses hitched to pickets near the road were killed outright, and a fellow by his automobile received a nasty gash in the side. He died almost immediately. Two other lads also received slight wounds. On inspection the bomb had made but a slight indentation in the road, while the force of the shell was felt on the sides, spreading and throwing the fragments of steel in a wide radius.

Further down the road were two Frenchmen manning a couple of artillery pieces when one blew up, adding to the toll of the dead in that short period of an afternoon. Shelling was continuous throughout the evening, and the night was never quiet. When we looked toward the Argonne wondering how our infantry was pushing through this barrage, as shelling and liquid fire poured in through the forest, the next day assured us the job was a stiff proposition. As for us, we had visions of being called into the mêlée.

On the second day the advance was slight with the Germans putting up a solid front and fighting with a resistance that unparalleled anything during the whole conflict. Their positions seemed impregnable; yet on the infantry went, leaving a trail of dead and dying. Our artillery now seemed to be raging with a deadlier blow and fighting hard to cut a path for the untiring doughboys. Tanks thundered on only to be brought to a sudden stop by the dense foliage and barbed wire. I later saw these tanks deserted in the forest, after becoming ensnared by the wire entanglements. At night the infantry engagements ceased, only to be followed up by bombers and much artillery action till morning. This barrage woke us with a roar that shook the trees from the very earth.

For the third day we battered and hammered with a vengeance at the slow retreating Germans, capturing prisoners and much booty, till finally, with one more determined effort, the Argonne Forest was cleared. For the first time in five days from our position as reserves, we saw the big guns moving forward, and then I knew the First Division had won. Yet we still drove ahead, leaving behind this famous Forest of the Argonne, our greatest prize of the war. Among the prisoners captured was one colonel whom I saw as he passed by in an officer's automobile. From him the following statement was made and sent to all units of the First Division.

"I received orders to hold my ground at all costs. The American barrage advanced toward my position, and the work of your Artillery was marvelous. The barrage was so dense that it was impossible for us to move out of our dug-outs. Following the barrage closely was the Infantry of the First Division. I saw them forge ahead, and I knew that all was lost. All night I remained in my dug-out hoping vainly that something would happen which would permit me to rejoin my army. This morning your troops found me and here I am, after four years of fighting, your prisoner.

"Yesterday I knew that the First Division was opposite us and I knew that we would have to fight our hardest of the war. The First Division is wonderful and the German Army knows it. We did not believe that within five years the Americans could develop a division like the First. The work of its Infantry and Artillery is worthy of the best armies of the world."

CFDAEF: 11

This tribute came from one of Germany's seasoned field officers. It was with great pleasure that we learned that even our enemies recognized the courage, valor, and efficiency of our troops. The work done by the First Division during the past few days will go down in history as one of the most memorable events which will live in the hearts of the American people in the generations to come.

After driving the Germans from the Argonne, each unit received the following from General Pershing: "The Allied troops are now engaged all along the Western Front in the largest combined movement of the war. It is of extreme importance that the 1st American Army drive forward with all possible force.

"There is evidence that the enemy is retiring from our own front.

"Our success must be followed up with the utmost energy, and pursuit continued to bring about the confusion and demoralization, and to prevent the enemy from forming his shattered forces.

"I am counting on the splendid spirit, dash, and courage of our Army to overcome all opposition. Our country expects nothing else."

CFDAEF:36

[Ed. Charles Edward Dilkes noted General Orders 20, 66, 201 and 232 and Commendation from Major General Liggett, which are included in the Appendix: 163+.]

Living History

AMERICAN OPERATIONS IN THE MEUSE-ARGONNE REGION:
OCTOBER 8, 1918[114]

[Extract]

After the deep advance of the First Army near here on October 4 and 5, the Germans continued to hold the edge of the Argonne Forest in this vicinity and from it kept up a continuous artillery fire directly along and in rear of the lines of the American units on this side of the river, inflicting heavy casualties.

In order to exploit the gains of the 1st and 28th Divisions on this side of the Argonne, to stop the artillery fire from the forest and to relieve a detachment of the 77th Division which had gone ahead of the rest of its division on October 2 and had been surrounded for several days in the Argonne Forest to the left war of here, it was decided to launch an attack from this vicinity straight at the German positions near Châtel-Chéhéry and Cornay. An attack in that direction would threaten the flank and rear of the hostile forces which were then holding the strong German second position out 3 miles to the left war of this point, and if successful would force the enemy to withdraw from that position and all of the Argonne Forest.

The 1st Division had consolidated its gains made on October 5 and had carried on active patrolling. It was assigned to the V Corps on October 7 preparatory to making a general attack with that corps. **On October 8 considerable fighting took place on the hills to the right of Montrefagne, one of the hills, Hill 269, being captured on that day by a battalion of 1st Division engineers.**

[Ed. Note: October 8 is the birthday of Charles Edward Dilkes.]

United States Army Center of Military History (1998), "American Armies and Battlefields in Europe: American Operations in the Meuse-Argonne Region," *United States Army in World War I,* version 2, CD-ROM disc 3 of 3: 227-230.

Operations near Sedan, November 6-7, 1918

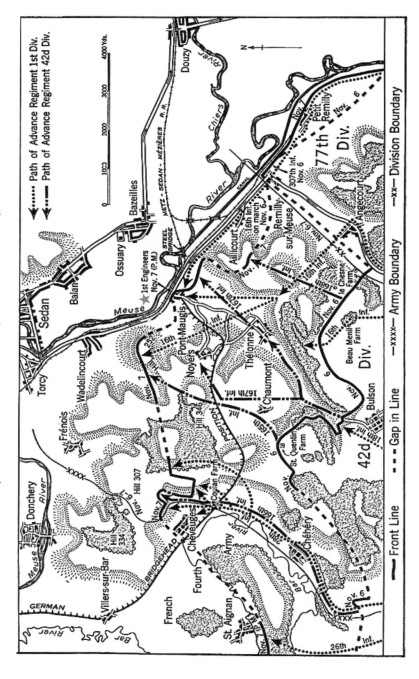

Figure 18: Map of Battle for Sedan[115]

SEDAN

On Friday, October 11th, at 3 o'clock the Division was relieved by the soldiers of the 42nd Division (Rainbow) who were as disgruntled going in as we were happy coming out. That afternoon we continued the march to Islettes, a camp constructed in one of the many dense forests in France. For the first time reports came that Turkey signed an armistice and Bulgaria was approaching towards this end.

Completely worn out as we were, this news was heralded with glad acclaim, and the march to Louppy le Petit the next day was made in more jovial spirits. For three days we tramped the roads, arriving there on October 16th.

This town, besides being in a sad state of disruption, could boast of possessing one of the few improvised shower baths that were greatly needed for the First Division at this time. We managed to indulge here in that rare sport called bathing. A general overhauling ensued, and a complete line of clothing was had by everyone. Here I enjoyed my first rabbit party, and in fact, many of these elaborate meals were prepared during our stay here—of course at our own expense. But we found this a good treat after we feasted for so long on hard-tack, slum,[116] and corn bill.[117]

Decked out in our new regalia, we assembled in a large open field for defensive drills, which was the signal—and the one that caused a relapse in spirit—for we knew now it was to the front again. The Division had looked forward to that much needed rest. On the 28th orders were received to move. We left Louppy le Petit on the 29th by trucks which convoyed us to Bois de Parois where we pitched our tents in the woods.

Sleeping in the woods was not so comfortable, as the nights now had the wintry touch to them, and staying warm was rather difficult. From here we went to Ivoiry and repaired roads near Cierges. Here we learned that Austria demanded peace. Things were beginning to look brighter now, and we had hopes that another entrance into the lines would be spared for us.

On November 1st we left Ivoiry to repair roads between Sommerance and Romagne. For three days this work was carried on untroubled by enemy shellfire. However, when [we were] about to retire one evening, shells began to break behind us and in the near by field known as our corral. After discovering some of our horses had been killed, a detachment was sent out to make an investigation. We knew the enemy was nowhere near us, for reports were just received that our troops lost all contact with them, and hence to have this barrage sent in our midst became a source of anxiety.

It was discovered that our infantry, in its dash after the swiftly retreating Germans, had missed capture of a detachment of Germans and an artillery gun. This investigating unit soon surrounded this enemy and took as prisoners six Boche who had concealed themselves in a dugout. Their ammunition was plentiful, and they, thinking their capture would mean death anyway, sought to cause as much destruction as possible before surrendering.

After almost completing our work on the roads here, word came to rejoin the regiment in the Bois de Romagne where immediate pursuit of the enemy would take place. Word was received that Austria signed an armistice. We looked forward to Germany signing, and my belief was that it would soon follow now that her allies had left her. For ten miles we marched and saw no trace of the Boche. On we rushed and still no sign of them. Still we pursued over rocky roads, through woods and over hills, and finally reached the bottom of the steep hill which leads to Stonne. We arrived there at nine o'clock on November 4th after a forced march of twenty miles. A steady drizzle set in. Rain-soaked and tired, we seemed to commence our ascent of this mountain to Stonne in a dazed sort of condition.

It was a rainy miserable night. Half way up we were held up as the Boche, in their hasty rush to escape, delayed our advance by undermining the hill, blowing a crater thirty feet deep, and demolishing half of the road. Troops were coming down; the hill was literally packed with men and animals crowding up, so we threw ourselves exhausted on the muddy bank, awaiting clearance of this congestion. For one hour we lingered when orders came to return to the foot of the hill again where further orders would be issued by the captain. At this point no one had the spirit to do anything, so fatigued were we.

We retraced our steps to the foot of the hill, where assembling about our captain we heard his dramatic speech dealing with the honor being extended us in assisting at the storming of the heights about Sedan. We received our orders to prepare to file in as support for the infantry on a hasty march to Sedan. The infantry was called from the lines along the Meuse River, where they awaited our coming to construct a bridge across the river to facilitate their passage and that of their artillery.

We now were held at Stonne, when at 12 o'clock the infantry reached us and took position ahead, ready for the thirty-mile hike to capture Sedan. Onward we pushed for two hours with no rest, and even now the five minutes we were given were because of the mining of the road leading through the forest. Here engineers were using all efforts to construct a bridge over these craters so our artillery and other wagons could follow. We slowly moved by this obstruction and then pushed forward at a rapid rate, many of the men falling by the wayside, and others sleeping while in a standing position.

At seven o'clock on the morning of November 7th, we reached Chemery. Here we allowed the 26th Infantry to be in full command of the road, while we filed behind marching on to Chehery. At Chehery the regiment halted, lying along the embankment by the side of the road. Our position now was one kilometer from a turn in the road and where the 26th Infantry, marching in squad column, met an onslaught from German machine guns. Immediately they formed a skirmish line and advanced, capturing the nest. We witnessed a terrific shelling of the town below us in the valley. This little village up to then was unharmed, but soon was completely wiped out. We noticed all these villages were flying a white flag from the top of their highest point, which was done because the inhabitants were informed by the Germans that the Americans were savages, shooting and shelling all

Living History

AMERICAN OPERATIONS IN THE MEUSE-ARGONNE REGION:
NOVEMBER 7, 1918[118]

On the afternoon of November 5 the I Corps was directed to capture Sedan, assisted on its right by the V Corps. As a result of a misconception in the V Corps of the exact intent of the orders, the 1st Division crossed the zone of action of the 77th Division and entered that of the 42d Division. This resulted in both the 1st and 42d Divisions operating in this general region on November 6 and 7.

Before daylight on November 7 a column of troops of the 1st Division captured a German wagon train in Pont-Maugis, partially mopped up the town in hand-to-hand fighting, and then moved up a little valley towards Thélonne. En route there it suffered heavily from fire from that hill, from across the Meuse River and from the south, but most of the column succeeded in joining other troops of its division near Thélonne. **Pont-Maugis was reentered by German troops but was retaken again about 2:00 o' clock in the afternoon by an engineer company of the 1st Division.**

During the morning of November 7 the 1st and 42d Divisions attacked the German bridgehead positions. After intense fighting, they succeeded in capturing these positions shortly after midday, and forced the German troops to retire still closer to Sedan. The American front line was then established on the Sedan side of Hill 252, after which patrols of the 42d Division advanced to within 100 yards of Wadelincourt.

The French desired, probably for sentimental reasons, to be the first to enter Sedan; so during the night of November 7-8 the positions on the hills were turned over to them. The left boundary of the First Army was at that time changed by the Allied Commander-in-Chief so that it ran in a northeasterly direction passing near Pont-Maugis.

United States Army Center of Military History (1998), "American Armies and Battlefields in Europe: American Operations in the Meuse-Argonne Region," *United States Army in World War I,* version 2, CD-ROM disc 3 of 3: 297-298.

villages with gas. The white flag was to notify us that the town was vacated by the Germans, and no resistance was to be expected from the town.

The shelling by the Huns continued for an hour or more, many shells coming dangerously close to wiping out artillery units led by horses galloping along the road. Bridges across streams were blown up, huge craters were formed in the roads after being dynamited, and telephone poles and wires were entangled across the roads—all obstructing the onrush of troops eager to capture this pre-eminent post "Sedan." A German automobile lay alongside the road completely demolished. This automobile was demolished by the Germans so no use could be made of it by the Americans. No doubt there was no time to repair this machine, so the Huns made a quick escape, blowing the machine apart first.

There was fighting to within the very gates of the city before the Division stopped. On the morning of November 8th, the Company started back to Stonne, as the French wished to have the honor of capturing Sedan. Since this relieved us from the line, we marched on to Stonne where we remained that night. It was there we learned officially of the German envoys arriving to sign the armistice. [Ed. Charles Edward Dilkes referred to General Order 26 and a Commendation from General C.P. Summerall, which are included in the Appendix: 167+.]

On the 10th we hiked to Sommauthe, remaining there for the night working on roads. The following day, November 11th, my Company broke camp again marching to Nouart. It was on this march at 10 a.m. a captain, riding swiftly past the column, shouted the glad tidings that the armistice was to be signed at 11 a.m.! Even now, trudging along with the same heavy pack, rifle, gas mask, etc., we could not believe the great conflict was at an end. There was no indication that this report was to be accepted as truth. So on we marched as unconcerned as to our destination and thinking about the next lines we were to enter. However, we kept tabs on the time. We now eagerly waited the approaching hour when all guns along the line were to cease firing.

True to the report at 11 a.m. not a shot was heard. Hostilities were at an end. As for me, once more visions of the gay white lights of old Broadway cheered me for the first time in two years. Our camp that night, where the whole Division concentrated, assumed the guise of a burning city. Rockets of all descriptions lighted the surrounding country; surplus hand grenades and rifle bullets helped celebrate this joyful occasion.

A Philadelphia newspaper, *Evening Public Ledger and the Evening Telegraph*, stated on Monday, November 11th, "The World War ended this morning at six o'clock Washington time ... Berlin was seized by the Revolutionists ... Marshall Foch, Supreme Allied Commander, gives official order for Allies to stop firing and cease hostilities." There is a five-hour time difference between Washington, D.C., and Paris; henceforth, we have the phrase "the 11th hour on the 11th day of the 11th month."

[THE WAR WAS OVER.]

We moved on the 12th to Bantheville, camping in shelter tents. Here we learned that the Kaiser fled to Holland and far away from our path of march. On the 15th we moved to French barracks, east of Verdun, marching in view of the ruined city and along the chain of those indomitable forts which were held so admirably by the French during the storming of this wonderful city. Our orders now were to proceed in haste as an advance guard during the march into and through German territory. At Abaucourt we joined a battalion of the 26th Infantry, and to the popular airs played by their band we began the long hike as a part of the Army of Occupation. On the 17th details were sent ahead to make reconnaissance, blowing up concrete pillars laid across the road to demolish tanks; bridges and engineer dumps were inspected.

The Company began its march first through Etain, then Rouvres, and many other French villages now free from the German yoke. We passed many freed Russian prisoners who were scampering still farther back into France and far enough away from any vestige of a German hand. Our journey was now through Lorraine territory, and we noticed this beautiful country was little touched by shells. We did find, however, that the huge trees lining the two sides of the roadway had deep gouges in them and were filled with explosive charges, ready to be felled across the roads if the fighting continued. Traces of this kind were evident all during our march through Lorraine.

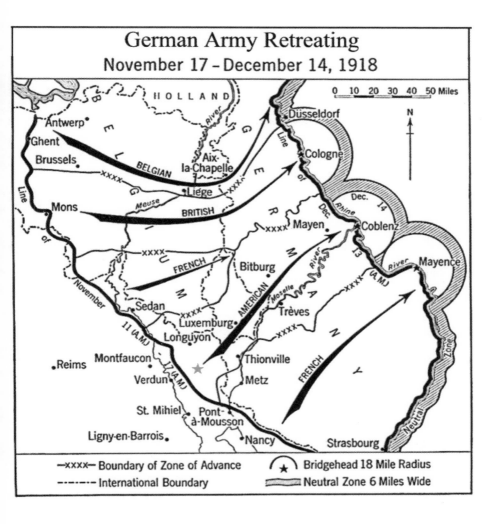

German Army Retreating
November 17 – December 14, 1918

Figure 19: Map of Armistice and the German Army Retreating[119]

German guns, purposefully broken over the trees, lay scattered along the way, showing their retreat was not to be hampered with any equipment. As village after village was passed through, the peasants noting our approach would assemble on both sides of the road, chanting "*La Marseillaise*,"[120] throwing kisses, and crying in joy at their deliverance. French flags were waving in the morning breeze from most every house while its companion, the grand old Red, White, and Blue, was seen unfurled in many places.

At three o'clock on November 20th we reached Thionville. Here the whole town came out, congregating around our Company, demanding practically that the captain let the men sleep in rooms they would provide in their houses. Every house must have some soldiers. I got nicely settled, and nothing would be done until I sat down to coffee, cake, and potatoes. This was continuous throughout the next day. Nothing pleased these people better than to have us partake of five or six meals a day. We set out again on the 21st, marching through Dudelange where the greeting was vociferous, people crying "*Vive la France, Vive l'Amérique*," arriving at Oelingen[121] at three o'clock, where we were billeted in houses for the night. The inhabitants here informed us the Germans left at ten o'clock, so we were but several hours behind this retreating army.

On the 22nd we reached and passed through Bettembourg and Schrassig and other cities of good size, where the inhabitants lined the sidewalks shouting for souvenirs such as a cap, a helmet, gas mask, etc. We finally arrived at Wolmerdingen in Luxembourg.[122] As we were the first American troops seen, our stay here from November 22nd until December 1st was a time of great rejoicing. Nothing was omitted in making us comfortable while the usual feasts were in evidence here. Our first sip of Moselle wine stimulated our wearisome bones. Here we drilled and got much time for cleaning up. At night our beloved Salvation Army[123] workers continued their ever thoughtfulness by serving hot chocolate and cake along the riverbank in the evening—a line of considerable length always formed.

On the morning of December 1st, being relieved from the advance guard, we crossed the bridge into Germany with the main body of troops, hiking down the Moselle River to a town called Ayl. Our treatment by the Germans was beyond expectations, for they, too, insisted upon our sitting at their table for every meal; and then, before going to bed, they brought us coffee and cake. Wine was plentiful. All along the Moselle River the steep hills flourished with grape vines which extended for miles. Each day was now a continuous march of twenty kilometers that wound in and out of this zigzagging Moselle River.

During this first week's march in December, I was compelled to fall behind, taking care of one lad completely exhausted. I was walking along slowly, when from a handsome residence a dignified German, brought to the roadway by the noise of troops passing, addressed me in French with the customary "*Bon jour!*" and asked if I would stop awhile, come in for wine, and rest. I accepted this opportunity to relieve myself of the heavy pack and found a few moments of solace in a luxurious office. The *Herr* German[124] bade his stenographer to get some wine at the same time offering me a cigar. Both favors were certainly appreciated. The conversation dwelt on the war in as far as America was concerned.

I bade him good-bye, and after leaving, I could not help but think of this kind hospitality given an enemy. This fellow was mighty friendly, and I judged that he felt that we Americans were friends and not enemies. It was a surprise also to note these handsome dwellings and how, for country homes, they far surpassed the French homes in towns of similar size. Our whole route now through Lorraine German territory was lined with these stately and handsome homes.

Each day we marched for ten or fifteen miles along the winding Moselle River, taking a ferry across here and there, passing through village after village which was situated along its banks. On December 7th we observed the first boat making its journey down this circuitous course and probably was the first boat doing so since the war began. We did not linger for long, however, since a bed was more pleasing to us at this time and was always something to which we looked forward.

Orders were issued that no man was to walk about alone. On the first night in one of these German towns, we were ordered to go about armed with rifle. After a few nights out this order ceased, for there was no sign of any hostile acts on the part of these people. On December 10th, after a wearisome journey of thirty-five kilometers, we arrived at a town called Bornich and mighty glad to learn but thirty miles from Coblenz. On December 13th the First Division crossed the bridge and entered the

Living History

ADVANCE OF THE 1ST DIVISION TOWARD GERMANY[125]

Crossing German Frontier

November 22, 1918.

Commanding General, Third Army

No. 2115 G-3. Allied Commander-in-Chief has fixed December 1 as date on which Allied troops will cross German frontier. Instructions will be sent November 23.

American zone includes bridgehead at COLOGNE [corrected to COBLENZ] and with axial line approximately marked by TREVES and COBLENZ approximately 70 kilometers in width.

By order:

CONNER.

United States Army Center of Military History (1998), "Military Operations of the American Expeditionary Forces," *United States Army in World War I,* version 2, CD-ROM disc 2 of 3, volume X, Part I, Preface: 136.

*****

As recorded in *A History of the 1st U.S. Engineers - 1st U.S. Division:*

From November 17 to December 1, companies "B" and "F" formed part of and marched with the advance guard of the two columns of the Division. They executed such engineer work as was necessary, including reconnaissances of roads, bridges, and dumps and the removal of obstacles in the line of march.

On December 1, the Regiment marched from Luxemburg into Germany. The Moselle was crossed at WOLMERDINGEN. Companies "C" and "E" now marched with the advance guards, relieving companies "B" and "F." From the 1st until the 13th, we marched down the tortuous Moselle Valley to COBLENZ.... On December 14, the Rhine was crossed.

Farrell, T. F. (Ed.). (1919). *A History of the 1st U.S. Engineers - 1st U.S. Division.* Coblenz, Germany: 53+.

city of Coblenz as the first Americans to enter as one contingent of the Army of Occupation. [Ed. Charles Edward Dilkes noted General Orders 203 and 204, which are included in the Appendix: 169+. Soldiers of the First Division were awarded the Victory Medal for their participation in the Meuse-Argonne Campaign, Appendix: 171.]

Figure 20: Zone of the American Army of Occupation[126]

U.S. ARMY OF OCCUPATION IN GERMANY

Everything was quiet as we crossed the long pontoon bridge[127] which spans the Rhine River into the city of Coblenz. There was no demonstration or opposition. The inhabitants cast but casual glances at us, as though it was an everyday occurrence for them to see soldiers marching along. They seemed indifferent to the whole situation, but perhaps they thought it was just an overnight stay. However, we were soon quartered in the classrooms of the huge Jesuit university, and I was immediately ordered for guard duty. I could only note the gayety that must prevail here by the many stragglers locked arm in arm passing on their way home from a nearby cabaret. Strains of a song from a hilarious quartet could be heard concluding with the usual American "Yow!"[128] Others would pass and begin dancing. Evidently their evening of dance was not finished at the cabaret so they chose the main highway to continue dancing, and it seemed always to be when they were opposite me, as if to say, "See what you are missing." I judge we may say it was a time for jubilation and celebration, and the Germans were numerous in this merriment, but again it was evident to them it would be their last.

We were not to stop here for long, so on the morning of December 14th we departed, marching to a town called Wirges, twenty-eight miles from Coblenz. Here the soldiers were quickly distributed about the neighboring dwellings. I shared the home of Herr Warner with four other men. The *Frau*[129] and *Herr* joined in to make us as comfortable as possible.

The usual hospitality was continued here as in France, and nothing would be but we sit down to as many meals as we could. In the evening after supper a stampede to fill our bed sacks with straw ensued. We placed these bed sacks in the living room ready for an extended stay in Germany. It was not long before we were thoroughly acclimated.

Well the army life that prevailed here was not relaxing.[130] Drills, hikes, inspections, and reviews were the daily routine. Often the Division would assemble to do honor to some high mogul irrespective of the weather, and all this certainly did not appeal to me. I considered my work finished with the signing of the armistice; now home and discharge were my cry. I arrived with the First in France, went into the lines with the First, was with the last division in the lines, and now, just think, the last to go home.[131] The thought of this grinds a peacetime soldier, and it sort of caused all my muscles to collapse. My mind could not even function except for thoughts of a scheme to frustrate this requirement to drag me out each day with a pack and rifle. Toting a gun and pack for a living stung me, while the hankering for once more to be a civilian certainly did not lesson my burden. Coming in for the evening, I was always primed for an argument with my friend Herr Warner when he, too, was ready and willing to discuss war and the present consequences.

Time dragged on till Christmas brought relief in a form of relaxation when we sampled the wine freely and partook of one fine meal. It was an elaborate meal that was composed of all the intricacy and finery of cooking our Frau Warner could bring forth. In the morning a large congregation assembled in the Catholic Church to hear Mass said in honor of the dead soldiers. This church was a large structure and of the same artistic design as we found in France.

Each day now we spent pursuing the usual "squads right" and "squads left." Our hopes for a relief were rudely shattered by the appearance of a thirty-piece band assigned to our regiment. These members had already embarked for America but were ordered from the steamer and sent to our regiment. That evening we had review, which I suppose was for the purpose of trying out our new band. The next night again we had review, and the next and the next and so on until the novelty wore off. Then the band was heard mostly at Sunday night concerts, playing for the benefit of the town in the public square.

On December 22, 1918, to cap the climax to all these drills, inspections, reviews, etc.—and on the coldest day one could experience—General Pershing and staff ordered the Division at Montabaur to stand for review. With full equipment we assembled on the hills while the General reviewed us from an opposite hill. Half frozen, standing around waiting for the General to appear, we were surely bewildered when the order came for coat collars down and gloves off. Now tell me, is there any sane person who would go out on a bitter cold day without gloves? Well we were forced to march so and carry a gun with a metal butt plate just because we were soldiers. Running the chance of a court-martial, I slipped my wristlets down over my half frozen fingers wishing Godspeed and much success to the review.

I here quote the sentiments of the volunteers after we reached Company quarters:[132]

> *"Darling I am coming back,*
> *With silver hairs among the black*
> *Now that Peace in Europe nears*
> *I'll be home in seven years.*
>
> *I'll drop in on you some night*
> *With my whiskers long and white*
> *Yes, the war is over, dear*
> *And we're going back I hear.*
>
> *Home again, with you once more*
> *Say by Nineteen Twenty-four*
> *Once by now I thought I'd be*
> *Sailing back across the sea.*
>
> *Back to where you sit and pine*
> *But I'm heading for the Rhine*
> *You can hear the MPs curse*
> *War is hell but Peace is worse.*
>
> *When the next war comes around*
> *In the front rank I'll be found*
> *I'll rush in again pell-mell*
> *Yes I will, I will like hell."*

Pay day came to our rescue on December 27th. We had been expecting our pay for days, and for days the old song was sung as was often sung on our marches to the lines in France:[133]

> *"Uncle Sam when he pays his infantry*
> *When he pays artillery*
> *When he pays his cavalry*
> *Then by gosh he locks up his treasury*
> *To hell with the ENGINEERS."*

That night we had our own feast, having the Frau fix up some rabbits—all of which were done in a very creditable manner. Of course, to forget our drills, hikes, parades, and reviews, we had to have wine. Strange to say, the next morning the Company's drill was a rabbit hunt. We formed a skirmish line and marched through the heavy brush. These expeditions were held regularly for a week, but I do not recall ever having caught a rabbit. One day we stirred up a young deer, but this deer hurdled the back of a man and got safely away.

We now awaited our passes that were in force. Many fellows were given permission to travel to Paris or other leave areas. Each day for four months I saw men after men take their leave and many with my Company, but half the time some of us were left out. I was annoyed since I was one of the first to put my name in. I had in mind my beloved sister [Marie-Louise] who answered the call, arriving in Paris in 1917. She gave her time, patience, and endurance with untiring interest to the American Soldiers' & Sailors' Club.[134] How well this organization is known among the A.E.F.[135] you have only to ask a soldier.

I received no permission as yet, and with the same grouchy attitude I went out each day for drill or inspection and every conceivable formation in the good book of the Army. Strict discipline was adhered to at all times, and even the Germans were attributing the militaristic epithet to us in counter to our voicing this epithet to them. One German was a volunteer like us and saw service on the Russian front. As he soon became familiar with our methods of playing sick to get off duty, he described their method of taking pepper so as to bring on a slight fever.

Many heated arguments we had with the Germans in whose homes we lived, but none of an antagonistic nature. One German firmly believed they were not whipped and even passed with approval the many outrages their army committed, with the exception of the invasion of Belgium, which he attributed to the Prussians.[136] The arguments always ended with, "Well,

Figure 21: Cartoon of History of the 1st Division in World War I[137]

the Germans will have to sign peace." "No, *Schwartzer*,"[138] he would say, "Germany never sign peace."

In spite of peace not having been signed yet, division after division had been sent home, but still the First remained. The first of the year found elaborate preparations under way for the carrying on of theatrical shows to travel about the occupied area. Through this enterprise many pleasant evenings were spent. Vaudeville entertainers, musical shows, dances, and such were presented through January and February. To relieve us from the monotony of drills during the day, on January 15th ground was broken for the construction of a rifle pit where each one would endeavor to become a marksman or expert rifleman. I think I got the booby prize.

Many unexpected incidents were happening now, such as orders coming that no man was to fraternize, that is, no man was to go out with the *frauleins*.[139] Another order stated that the Germans were not to sell schnapps[140] to the men; another that all men must have their hair cut and submit to inspection so that the inspecting officer could not catch a hold of it in the front. This all lasted one week. Soon every man had a girl, schnapps was bought as usual, and the hair was cut to suit the man.

For the rest of the month we again took up drills, inspections, and reviews, parading on January 24th to Montabaur for the grand annual review, I suppose. Anyway we were sick of it all and were glad when pay day came on February 2nd. Now a new idea crept into camp which was to organize schools in various branches: drawing, mathematics, English, etc. This idea lasted about one week. No, only one suggestion was worth listening to and that was to go home.

The officers, I presume, thought I needed a little divergence for they chose me to unload a freight car of coal ... and soft coal at that. I presented a pretty sight when I arrived home. After we burned this soft coal for a couple of days, the Frau cleaned out the stove. This job was so mean that she, too, became covered with coal soot. The coal soot did not prevent our enjoying the regimental show at night, and a very creditable showing was made.

One feature will stand out as a big credit to the Army during this Occupation and this was the opportunity offered a few to attend either a college in England or a university in Paris. As most men were clamoring for home, there was but slight inducement towards this notion. Three or four men took the offer and went.

Through the month of February a horse show, musical shows, moving pictures, and banquets helped relieve the monotony of a soldier's life. On the 12th the Company celebrated its one-year and a half in Europe with a banquet.

The 13th brought a letter from Sis stating she had written to my commanding officer for my leave to visit Paris. I settled back and awaited what effect her letter would have. Up to the 10th of March not a word and no sign of a pass.

I now got in touch with headquarters, and although they assured me that they would pass my request through, it required an OK from my Company commander. His permission I could not get and was told I must wait my turn. March dragged itself along accompanied with drills, musical shows, and peace talks. April came and still there was no hope of returning to the States. In fact it seemed this month was devoted to a strenuous campaign to reenlist men. Smooth talking shave-tails[141] visited all units and endeavored by their carefully studied campaign to inveigle these soldiers to sign away their life to another three-year hitch in the Army. Their flourishing propositions did appeal to a few, but the big inducements to these were the frauleins. The fifteenth of April brought relief. The Captain called me from the ranks, and after handing me a letter which he claimed should be rewritten, informed me that I may state in it that I would receive my pass on the 16th. I was to write this letter as one to my sister wherein I was to say that I would go to a higher authority for my pass; but I was afraid such a letter would hurt my chances of ever going. The captain took exception to my line of reasoning. So I wrote the letter, which had its intended effect.

On the 16th the first step towards my goal was made: my journey for Paris began. Arriving in Coblenz, I found all the soldier tourists assembled in the Y.M.C.A.[142] Each group was waiting for his train. To the Red Cross we must take off our hats for it was they who in an untiring manner served all with whatever we could eat and as much as we could devour. It was a supreme moment to note the cheerful manner and willing attitude they showed; vividly it brought to mind this same spirit which was continually shown to us during the hard grind of the war, never tiring in their unceasing favors.

After awhile a fellow enlivened things by playing the piano, and with the group of soldiers surrounding me, I gave bent to my elation over this trip by clogging. It was not my intention to make myself conspicuous, but somehow or other I forgot the audience, and more to amuse myself I started to move my feet. On stopping I received a jolt by way of applause, which brought me to my feet again, and nothing would be but I submit to the encore. You would be surprised how easy it is to amuse a crowd who were in jovial spirits due in no doubt to these few days of rest.

The announcement of the arrival of my train came to my rescue. All aboard, and the first step towards Paris commenced. After experiencing the usual delays at transfer points, blocks, etc., for three days, I finally rolled into La Gare de Paris on the 19th. It was too late now to make inquiries, and the little French I knew would not help me in telephoning, so a bottle of wine, a wild ride about the gay white way of Paris, and a good night's rest could get me ready for the gladsome visit in the morning.

By the time the sun showed itself in all its glory, I had hailed a taxi and was speeding along merrily to the American Soldiers' & Sailors' Club on the Rue Royale. I think I took five steps at a time and, after almost colliding with a major or colonel or other, gave a knock on the door. I pulled the latch and peeped in and there, after two years of almost inexhaustible energy, untiring in her endeavors with unshaken determination, stood that pretty little picture of my sister, which suddenly was transformed into a reality when our glances met. Immediately I declared a holiday. We two strolled the Garden of Elysée, learning all the news that lay dormant for these long years; and I learned of the great work that was carried on, which brought back my good spirits once more. Now for the first time I had peace of mind and body. If possible, I would now sail for home knowing my work was completed.

Figure 22: American Soldiers' & Sailors' Club Card
(Marie-Louise Dilkes)

Much to my regret this time was all I saw of Marie-Louise; but now that I am leaving Paris, it did not cause the interest my sister had in me during the whole war to cease. Later on, while holding the lines ready to force our way into the very heart of Germany if peace failed, I was recipient of many gifts from Sis. The gifts seemed to arrive always when mostly needed, as though Heaven Herself sent them. These gifts from a big heart brought to my mind the time we sat in her apartment and she told me of her experiences. Then I wondered how this little mite did it: two years ago, when at the height of hostilities, when all Paris and in fact the whole world had no thoughts but of the war, she fought obstacle after obstacle; and everything she conquered successfully, with that same dogged determination and will power as followed her from the shores of America. I found that after two years just as big a battle had been fought right here. As I sat before her, I saw that joy of the conqueror with the inscribed motto, and which she presented to me on leaving, "*Quand Même.*"[143]

Arriving at my command on the 23rd of April, I was not surprised to still find the men undergoing the same old grind, "squads east" and "squads west." Falling into this reality suddenly after ten days of freedom and gayety, free from cares and worry among the hustle and bustle of Paris, was a plunge that almost undermined my whole system. I survived this sunken feeling sufficiently to fall in with my Company as we prepared for our departure; we were to take up positions along the front lines in order to subdue the Germans into signing the much desired PEACE PACT.

For months we heard of the treacherous dickering of the peace envoys, bluffing and postponing, meeting again then adjourning, mocking and laughing with no idea or attempt at signing, hoping to soon outwit the conferences and pocket all their advantages. That the Allied representatives were now becoming impatient became evident when orders were sent for immediate mobilization along the neutral border. Hence on June 1st we took our position along this line, presenting a continuous battlefront with our Allies across the heart of Germany. We pitched tents in an open field, and I can tell you that the feeling at this time was so intense that if the order came to advance, Germany would have experienced the bitterest warfare that ever was waged. You have only to be with a regular army unit to appreciate what would have occurred.

A message sent on June 7, 1919, by Major General E. F. McGlachlin, Jr., Division commander, will give somewhat of an idea as to the disposition of the armies as we held the lines waiting for the signing of peace:

"German eyes look and see, Boche ears listen and hear, Hun lips tell all the half-truths and lies and only those truths calculated to accomplish their particular selfish objects.

"Our enemy still attempts always to impose his ideas on the world.

"Given every opportunity to avoid the war, he insists that he was not responsible.

"Beaten by Allied arms under American impetus, he denies that he was defeated but claims that he was deceived.

"Entering Belgium contrary to sacred promise, he avers, untruthfully, that a hostile nation did so first.

"Determined at the beginning to force his will upon all peoples not only for the power and grandeur and enrichment of Germany but for the fatal impoverishment of other nations, at the height of his successes he announced a pitiless policy of punishment of those who were fighting against him. Far beyond the requirements of military necessity, he killed American women and children through his underseas piracy, killed and maimed English women and children through bombardment of undefended places, destroyed French mines beyond repair for fifteen years, and ruined and stole Belgian machinery for no purpose except to delay resumption of industry that his own might more greatly prosper.

"Having through greed inflicted great losses upon us and our Allies, he now whines and weeps and wrings his hands that he is called upon for reparation in kind, though not in measure, for his misdeeds. He cries out against the diminution of war power imposed upon him to remove his serious menace to peace, not to punish him.

"As during the war by bribery, corruption, spying, stealth, secret destruction, lies, theft, violence, murder, violation of women, slavery, cruelty to children and old men and women, he made himself the horror of the world; now by his insolence, bluff, lies, appeals for sympathy, he makes himself contemptible. Contemptible, his might is no longer to be feared though he is dangerous. He is dangerous because without conscience he conducts an organized unscrupulous campaign to deny his unmeasured crimes, to create mutual distrust between the Allies, to make us suspicious of each other, to plant in our minds seeds of doubt of our principles, our institutions, and our President, to gain sympathy for his future imaginary distress.

"In that organized campaign the people among whom, through necessity, we live play their parts. By little welcome favors, by insistence, by repetition, by making a friend here and another there they attempt to force their wedges of argument, disclaim, pleading, suspicion, and distrust to break our conviction in the righteousness of our cause, the unworthiness of theirs.

"There is nothing consistent between German public motive and American spirit and ideals. There is nothing in our soldierly duty requiring or authorizing us to convert our enemy to our beliefs. There is everything

Living History

ACTIVITIES OF ARMY OF OCCUPATION: MAY 1919

[EXTRACT]

In May division commanders are held directly responsible for training. May 6, the 90th Div. is released to S. 0. S. and on May 8 those units of 6th Div. in Third Army area are also released. May 11, the IV and VII Corps are discontinued and the 4th and 5th Divs. released to the S.0.S.; the 3d Div. is transferred from IV to III Corps. May 14, plans of operations submitted by Marshal Foch to Third Army commander in event that GERMANY should refuse to sign the peace treaty. May 17, military police units, operating under civil affairs officers, take over control of such areas as divisions evacuate. May 20, Marshal Foch directs Allied commanders to dispatch troops toward WEIMAR and BERLIN from MAYENCE, COBLENZ, and COLOGNE, if peace treaty is not signed. May 22, Third Army issues its plan of advance, effective May 30, in view of the impending emergency. May 26, Operations Section, G. H. Q., A. E. F., recommends that one regiment with necessary auxiliaries, totaling in all about 7,000 troops, be the American contribution to any further occupation of German territory by the Allies. **May 27, Marshal Foch informs Gen. Pershing that Supreme War Council desires Allied Armies be made ready immediately to resume active operations against the Germans.**[144]

United States Army Center of Military History (1998), "American Occupation of Germany," *United States Army in World War I,* version 2, CD-ROM disc 2 of 3, Volume XI: 144.

in our soldierly duty requiring us to keep faithfully our own beliefs, to be loyal to our Allies, and to sustain our American traditions and morale.

"Let us see everything, hear everything, of value to our cause, say nothing to our enemy. Let us present and maintain our honor, perform exactly our duty, devote ourselves loyally to our country."

CFDAEF: 50

To sum all this up, the orders were that if the advance took place, to have no obstructions in our way, and, in fact, I do not think there would have been much mercy shown. The old saying among the troops still hung on: "Hoboken via Berlin." However, much to our relief, the cooling of our frenzied feeling was hastened by the ratification of Peace by the German National Assembly at Weimar, Germany, on July 9, 1919. Hence my experience of war came to a close.

Now that the end of all hostilities has come, I can only feel elated over the idea of going home soon. At this time there is great reason for our jubilee because we knew the feeling our esteemed General John J. Pershing held towards the First Division when on July 17, 1919, at London he delivered a speech from which an extract is here quoted.

"You will recall that when our 1st Division entered the battle line and fought the small though brilliant battle—the first as an independent command—at Cantigny, that the success which attended the attack not only set an example for future American divisions to follow, but really had an electrifying effect through the Allied lines and gave new hope to the armies."

He concluded with the thought, "The armistice stopped the First Division once; the signing of Peace stopped it a second time; German soldiers never stopped it."

Edwin L. James,
War Correspondent,
New York Times

CFDAEF: 55

Living History

ACTIVITIES OF ARMY OF OCCUPATION: DECEMBER 19, 1918 - JULY 2, 1919

193-33.1: Fldr. A; Operations Report[145]

Third Army, A.E.F., No. 46
June 18, 1919—10 h.

I. ESTIMATE OF THE SITUATION:

The Armistice having been provisionally renounced by the Allied and Associated Powers contingent only upon the non-acceptance by GERMANY of the proposed Treaty of Peace before June 23, 1919, it has become necessary to concentrate and prepare our forces for the anticipated resumption of the advance into GERMANY.

As no great resistance to our forward movement is expected, we may, by a rapid movement of our advance troops, seize important centers and lines of supply and communication far to the east of the present limit of the bridgehead, thus providing for an extensive forward movement upon further orders from the Allied Commander-in-Chief.

II. OWN MOVEMENTS AND CHANGES DURING PERIOD:

Third Army: The Third Army Composite Regiment entrained June 15 for Pershing Stadium near PARIS.

The 4th Division was ordered to reequip and prepare for active service June 18.

The 3d Division (less III Corps Reinforced Brigade] was relieved from duty with the III Corps June 17, by Field Order No. 8, Third Army Headquarters, and ordered to assemble along the RHINE in readiness for forward movement.

The III Corps Reinforced Brigade was concentrated June 18, at MAYEN and NIEDERMENDIG prepared for entrainment.

The 3d Field Artillery Brigade began June 16, a practice march toward the LUXEMBURG - GERMAN frontier designed as a test for motorized artillery.

1st Division: The infantry regiments of the 1st Division moved June 18 to positions in the close vicinity of towns. The artillery of the 1st Division remained in place near assembly positions.

2d Division: Regiments of the 2d Division moved June 18 to areas in close vicinity of towns.

MALIN CRAIG,
Chief of Staff.

United States Army Center of Military History (1998), "American Occupation of Germany," *United States Army in World War I*, version 2, CD-ROM disc 2 of 3, Volume XI: 123.

Living History

CORPS OF 1st ENGINEERS IN WORLD WAR I[146]

Regiments, Battalions, Companies

Unit Designation and Redesignation	Organization		Stations in United States		Overseas		Demobilization		Remarks
	Month and Year	Place	Month and Year	Place	From--	To--	Month and Year	Place	
1st Engineers (sapper[1] regiment)	Organised[2] 1916		April 1917...	Washington Bks., D.C.					Component of 1st Division
			August 1917	Port of Embarkation, Hoboken	August 1917				
	Returned from overseas		August 1919	Camp Mills, N.Y.		August 1919			
	Took station		September 1919	Camp Meade, MD					
	Relocated		October 1919	Camp Zachary Taylor, KY					Active through 1919

[1]A soldier employed as a member of an army corps of engineers and engaged in the construction of fortifications, trenches, or tunnels that approach or undermine enemy positions.

[2]Organized

United States Army Center of Military History (1998), "Order of Battle of the United States Land Forces in the World War,"
United States Army in World War I, version 2, CD-ROM disc 3 of 3, vol. 3: part 3, Zone of the Interior: Directory of Troops: 337.

G. H. Q.
AMERICAN EXPEDITIONARY FORCES,

GENERAL ORDERS }
No. 38-A.   }

FRANCE, *February 28, 1919.*

MY FELLOW SOLDIERS:

Now that your service with the American Expeditionary Forces is about to terminate, I can not let you go without a personal word. At the call to arms, the patriotic young manhood of America eagerly responded and became the formidable army whose decisive victories testify to its efficiency and its valor. With the support of the nation firmly united to defend the cause of liberty, our army has executed the will of the people with resolute purpose. Our democracy has been tested, and the forces of autocracy have been defeated. To the glory of the citizen-soldier, our troops have faithfully fulfilled their trust, and in a succession of brilliant offensives have overcome the menace to our civilization.

As an individual, your part in the world war has been an important one in the sum total of our achievements. Whether keeping lonely vigil in the trenches, or gallantly storming the enemy's stronghold; whether enduring monotonous drudgery at the rear, or sustaining the fighting line at the front, each has bravely and efficiently played his part. By willing sacrifice of personal rights; by cheerful endurance of hardship and privation; by vigor, strength and indomitable will, made effective by thorough organization and cordial co-operation, you inspired the war-worn Allies with new life and turned the tide of threatened defeat into overwhelming victory.

With a consecrated devotion to duty and a will to conquer, you have loyally served your country. By your exemplary conduct a standard has been established and maintained never before attained by any army. With mind and body as clean and strong as the decisive blows you delivered against the foe, you are soon to return to the pursuits of peace. In leaving the scenes of your victories, may I ask that you carry home your high ideals and continue to live as you have served—an honor to the principles for which you have fought and to the fallen comrades you leave behind.

It is with pride in our success that I extend to you my sincere thanks for your splendid service to the army and to the nation.

Faithfully,

John J. Pershing

Commander in Chief.

OFFICIAL:
ROBERT C. DAVIS,
Adjutant General.

Copy furnished to Pvt Charles E. Dilkes

H. B. Vaughan, Jr.

Capt., Engrs., U.S.A.
Commanding.

Figure 23: Farewell from General Pershing[147]

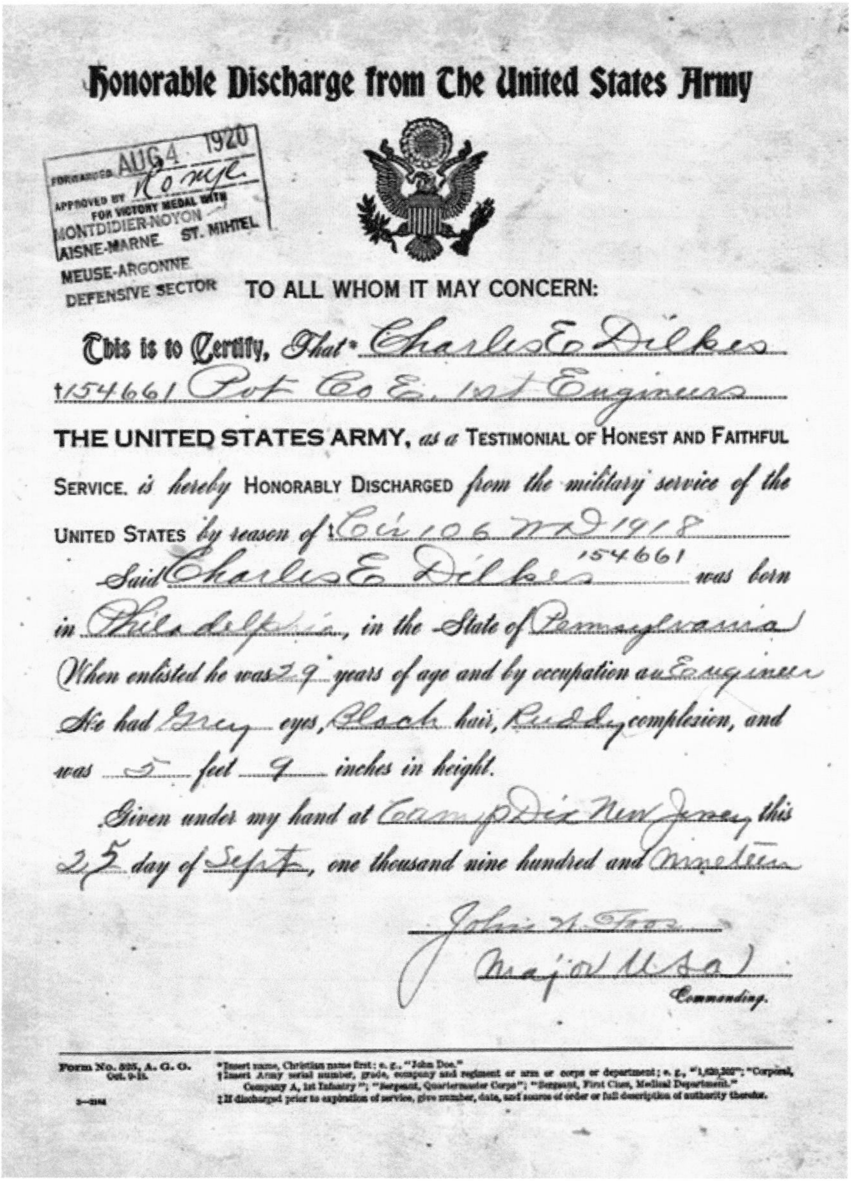

Honorable Discharge from The United States Army

TO ALL WHOM IT MAY CONCERN:

This is to Certify, That *Charles E. Dilkes* †154661 Pvt Co E. 1st Engineers

THE UNITED STATES ARMY, as a Testimonial of Honest and Faithful Service. is hereby Honorably Discharged from the military service of the United States by reason of *Cir 106 WD 1918*

Said *Charles E. Dilkes* 154661 was born in *Philadelphia*, in the State of *Pennsylvania* When enlisted he was *29* years of age and by occupation an *Engineer* He had *Grey* eyes, *Black* hair, *Ruddy* complexion, and was *5* feet *9* inches in height.

Given under my hand at *Camp Dix New Jersey* this *25* day of *Sept*, one thousand nine hundred and *nineteen*

John N. Fox
Major USA
Commanding.

Form No. 525, A. G. O.
Oct. 9-18.

*Insert name, Christian name first; e. g., "John Doe."
†Insert Army serial number, grade, company and regiment or arm or corps or department; e. g., "1,620,302"; "Corporal, Company A, 1st Infantry"; "Sergeant, Quartermaster Corps"; "Sergeant, First Class, Medical Department."
‡If discharged prior to expiration of service, give number, date, and source of order or full description of authority therefor.

FORWARDED AUG 4 1920
No mjl.
APPROVED BY
FOR VICTORY MEDAL WITH
MONTDIDIER-NOYON
AISNE-MARNE   ST. MIHIEL
MEUSE-ARGONNE
DEFENSIVE SECTOR

Figure 24: Honorable Discharge

POSTSCRIPT

We include the poem "Gunga Din," a favorite of Charles Edward Dilkes and a copy of which we found among the artifacts he saved, as it may have reflected on some feelings from his war experience. It is written by Rudyard Kipling[148] whose only son was killed in World War I. The poem tells of the courage of an Indian boy who is shot while carrying water to British soldiers in British India during the Thuggee uprising. It was first published in the United States in 1890 in *The National Observer* and later in *Barrack-Room Ballads*.

"Gunga Din"

You may talk o' gin and beer
When you're quartered safe out 'ere,
An' you're sent to penny-fights an' Aldershot it;
But when it comes to slaughter
You will do your work on water,
An' you'll lick the bloomin' boots of 'im that's got it.
Now in Injia's sunny clime,
Where I used to spend my time
A-servin' of 'Er Majesty the Queen,
Of all them blackfaced crew
The finest man I knew
Was our regimental bhisti, Gunga Din.

141

He was "Din! Din! Din!
You limpin' lump o' brick-dust, Gunga Din!
Hi! slippery hitherao!
Water, get it! Panee lao!
You squidgy-nosed old idol, Gunga Din."

The uniform 'e wore
Was nothin' much before,
An' rather less than 'arf o' that be'ind,
For a piece o' twisty rag
An' a goatskin water-bag
Was all the field-equipment 'e could find.
When the sweatin' troop-train lay
In a sidin' through the day,
Where the 'eat would make your bloomin' eyebrows crawl,
We shouted "Harry By!"
Till our throats were bricky-dry,
Then we wopped 'im 'cause 'e couldn't serve us all.

It was "Din! Din! Din!
You 'eathen, where the mischief 'ave you been?
You put some juldee in it
Or I'll marrow you this minute
If you don't fill up my helmet, Gunga Din!"

'E would dot an' carry one
Till the longest day was done;
An' 'e didn't seem to know the use o' fear.
If we charged or broke or cut,
You could bet your bloomin' nut,
'E'd be waitin' fifty paces right flank rear.
With 'is mussick on 'is back,
'E would skip with our attack,
An' watch us till the bugles made "Retire",
An' for all 'is dirty 'ide
'E was white, clear white, inside
When 'e went to tend the wounded under fire!

It was "Din! Din! Din!"
With the bullets kickin' dust-spots on the green.
When the cartridges ran out,

You could hear the front-files shout,
"Hi! ammunition-mules an' Gunga Din!"

I shan't forgit the night
When I dropped be'ind the fight
With a bullet where my belt-plate should 'a' been.
I was chokin' mad with thirst,
An' the man that spied me first
Was our good old grinnin', gruntin' Gunga Din.
'E lifted up my 'ead,
An' he plugged me where I bled,
An' 'e guv me 'arf-a-pint o' water—green:
It was crawlin' and it stunk,
But of all the drinks I've drunk,
I'm gratefullest to one from Gunga Din.

It was "Din! Din! Din!
'Ere's a beggar with a bullet through 'is spleen;
'E's chawin' up the ground,
An' 'e's kickin' all around:
For Gawd's sake git the water, Gunga Din!"

'E carried me away
To where a dooli lay,
An' a bullet come an' drilled the beggar clean.
'E put me safe inside,
An' just before 'e died:
"I 'ope you liked your drink", sez Gunga Din.
So I'll meet 'im later on
At the place where 'e is gone—
Where it's always double drill and no canteen;
'E'll be squattin' on the coals
Givin' drink to poor damned souls,
An' I'll get a swig in hell from Gunga Din!

Yes, Din! Din! Din!
You Lazarushian-leather Gunga Din!
Though I've belted you and flayed you,
By the livin' Gawd that made you,
You're a better man than I am, Gunga Din!

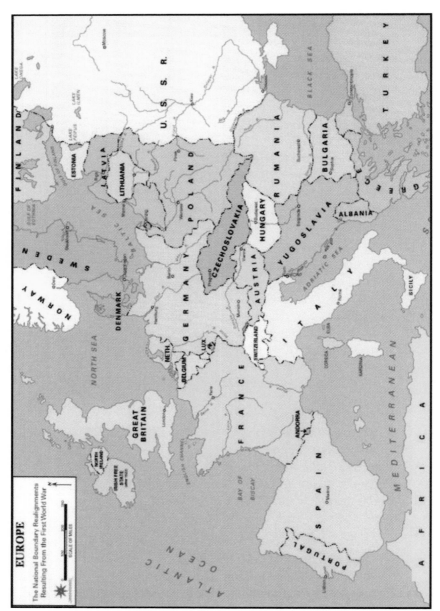

Figure 25: Map of Europe 1919: Post World War I[149]

APPENDIX

GENERAL ORDERS AND COMMENDATIONS

FIRST DIVISION

Lunéville-Sommerviller Sector

General Order #67

Headquarters, First Division,

American Expeditionary Forces.

France, November 23, 1917.

The troops of the First Division have completed their first tour of duty at the front. The casualties have been few as was expected in a quiet sector: fourteen killed, thirty-four wounded and eleven captured by the enemy. But the many discomforts, inconveniences and trials always incident to service at the front have been faced in a fine, uncomplaining spirit which speaks well for the soldierly qualities of the men. The Division Commander wishes to congratulate the soldiers of the Division upon their excellent conduct and cheerful demeanor during the past month at the front and particularly during the long, hard weeks of preliminary training in the cold and mud. He believes there are few occasions in the past where American soldiers have worked as hard and have endured as cheerfully so many discomforts and difficulties as have the men of this Division since landing in France.

We are now starting on the final period of training. Weather conditions will make it a peculiarly hard and trying one. The Division Commander feels that he can depend on every individual soldier to meet this situation with the same fortitude and resolution that he has heretofore displayed and to do his utmost to bring to a successful and speedy conclusion the preparation of this command to take its place, as a unit, in the first line in a manner to reflect credit and honor upon our country.

Wm. L. Sibert,

Major General, U.S.A.

Commanding.

CFDAEF: 14

Toul-Ansauville Sector

General Order #119

Headquarters, 1st Army,

32nd Army Corps Staff,

3rd Bureau 1030/3.

March 2, 1918.

On the 1st of March at daybreak, the enemy pulverized the first line trenches and dugouts occupied by the right of the 18th American Regiment with a heavy fire of minnenwerfers[150] and 210's. They then attacked in six columns under the protection of a rolling barrage. All instructions that had been given had been faithfully carried out. The Americans withdrew to the edge of the zone under fire, and then delivered a strong counter attack. The Boche realized the force of the American blow; he retreated to his position, leaving on the spot fifteen dead (of which two were officers). They also left four men to be taken as prisoners. The troops of the 32nd Army Corps, proud to be fighting by the side of generous sons of the Great Republic[151] who have hastened to support France, and, with her, to hasten the freedom of the world, will understand by this example of superb courage and coolness the full meaning of the promises made by the entry into the conflict of their new brother-in-arms.

The General commanding the 32nd Army Corps heartily congratulates the First American Division and in particular the 3rd Battalion of the 18th Infantry as well as the American Artillery whose precise and opportune action contributed to the success.

General Passaga
The General Commanding the 32nd Army Corps.

CFDAEF: 16

Tribute to Artillery Brigade During Action on March 11

Headquarters, First Division,

American Expeditionary Forces.

France, March 11, 1918.

I wish to express to you and your officers and men of your command my appreciation of the efficiency of your work in the raids just completed. The accuracy and effectiveness of the fires of your guns had enabled the raiding detachments to perform their missions without interference by the enemy and without the loss of a man, and has undoubtedly inflicted heavy losses on the enemy in addition to destroying his fortifications. The infantry has been inspired with great confidence by the assurance of insight and effective support by the artillery. Please communicate my congratulations to your command.

Robert L. Bullard,
Major General, N.A.
CFDAEF: 17

Tribute from General Marchand, Commanding the 10th Colonial

> Armee - 2nd Corps d'Armee Colonial,
> 10th Division Coloniale,
> Secteur Postal 167.
> 3rd Bureau, 21 Mars 1918.

General Marchand, Commandant of the 10th D.I.C., very warmly thanks the Artillery of the First Division for the help that it gave on the morning of March 20th against the raid launched by the enemy east of Apremont. The American Artillery opened its fire with a rapidity that is worthy of praise and which is proof of its vigilance and a warrant of its excellent training and instructions.

A few days ago our Artillery had the honor and pride to work for the First Division. Yesterday the American Artillery honored us with its work. The voice of our guns, American and French, has sealed in both ways the pact of union and confidence that is in all of our Allies' and soldiers' hearts.

> Marchand.
> CFDAEF: 17

General Order #123

> 32e Corps d'Armee.
> Etat-Major.
> 3e Bureau, April 4, 1918.

As the First Division leaves for battle, the officers, non-commissioned officers and soldiers of the 32nd Army Corps salute their brothers in arms, whose bravery they have admired.

They congratulate them on being privileged to write in the battle of nations the first page in the history of the sons of the Great Republic coming to fight on the soil of France for the triumph of Liberty.

This page will be glorious.

> Passaga.
> Commanding General, 32nd Army Corps.
> CFDAEF: 18

General Order #16

Headquarters, First Division,

American Expeditionary Forces.

France, April 2, 1918.

First. The commanding general of the 32nd French Army Corps has expressed in orders his approbation of the conduct of the Division while in this sector.

Second. The character of the service which the Division is now about to undertake, however, demands enforcement of a stricter discipline and the maintenance of a higher standard of efficiency than any heretofore required of us.

Third. From now on troops of this command will be held at all times to the strictest observation of that rigid discipline, in camp and upon the march, which is essential to their maximum efficiency on the day of battle.

Fourth. This order will be read by all organization commanders to the men of their command.

By command of Major General Bullard.

Campbell King, Chief of Staff.

CFDAEF: 18

The Storming of Cantigny

General Order #24

Headquarters, First Division,

American Expeditionary Forces.

France, June 3, 1918.

The following has been received by the Division Commander from the Commander-in-Chief and is published for the information of all concerned:

"Please accept my hearty congratulations upon the marked success of the attack made by your Division this morning upon Cantigny. Extend to all concerned my warm appreciation of the splendid spirit displayed and the well-ordered fashion in which the details of the plan were carried out. This engagement, though relatively small, marks a distinct step forward in American participation in the war.

With sincere regards, I remain,

Very cordially yours,

John J. Pershing."

By Command of Major General Bullard.

H.K. Loughry,

Major, F.A., Division Adjutant.

CFDAEF: 21

Montdidier-Noyon Campaign[152]
June 9–13, 1918

The Battle for Cantigny was rolled into the Montdider-Noyon Campaign. General Pershing wrote in *My Experiences in the World War* that the Cantigny sector at the end of May "was very active, with artillery fire unusually heavy, and the preparations for the attack by the 1st Division were carried out under great difficulty.[153] Many casualties occurred during the construction of jumping-off trenches, emplacements, and advance command posts. The 28th Infantry, under Colonel Hanson E. Ely, designated for the assault, was reinforced by tanks, machine guns, engineers, and other special units.

"On the morning of May 28th, after a brief artillery preparation, the infantry advanced on a front of a mile and a quarter. The village of Cantigny and the adjacent heights were quickly taken, relatively heavy casualties inflicted on the enemy, and about 240 prisoners captured. Our troops behaved splendidly and suffered but slight loss in the actual attack.

"The Germans' reaction against this attack was extremely violent as apparently he was determined at all cost to counteract the excellent effect the American success would produce upon the Allies. Under cover of this bombardment, several counterattacks were made by the enemy, but our young infantrymen stood their ground and broke up every attempt to dislodge them. The 28th Infantry sustained severe casualties and had to be reinforced by a battalion each from the 18th and 26th Infantry regiments."

The German General Ludendorff followed up his stalled Aisne offensive with a small-scale drive in the Montdidier – Noyon sector on June 9, 1918. The 21st German Division attacked the French on a twenty-three mile front extending from Montdidier to the Oise River. The French anticipated the assault and contained it after a nine-mile penetration by the Germans, counterattacking strongly. The fighting was over by June 12th, and the enemy had little to show for the heavy losses incurred. No large American units were in the immediate vicinity of this action, although the 1st Division at Cantigny was subjected to artillery fire and diversionary raids.

Soldiers of the 1st Division were awarded the Victory Medal for participation in the Montdidier-Noyon Campaign.

Figure 26: U.S. Army History of the Montdidier-Noyon Campaign

Aisne-Marne Operation

General Order #9

Headquarters, Third Army Corps,

American Expeditionary Forces.

France, July 23, 1918.

On the morning of July 18th, after forty-eight hours of exhausting, continuous almost sleepless movement, the 3rd Army Corps joined battle with the enemy. In your great offensive you stood beside the best Veteran French Troops, our Allies, and sustained, nay, did honor to the name American. Our Allies, your commanders, the Army of the United States and the whole nation are proud and will boast of your deeds and the deeds of those brave men, our beloved comrades, who at your side in the last five days have fallen paying the last sacrifice of soldiers. Now and for the future let us resolve that those our Allies and our people shall not trust in us in vain and, in the words of Lincoln, "That these our comrades shall not have died in vain."

By command of Major General Bullard.

A. W. Bjornstad,

Brigadier General, G.S., Chief of Staff.

CFDAEF: 25

Tribute from Major General Reed,
Commanding the 15th Scottish Division

To General Officer Commanding,
July 24, 1918.
1st American Division.

I would like, on behalf of all ranks of the 15th Scottish Division, to express to you personally, to your staff, and to all our comrades in your splendid Division our most sincere thanks for all that has been done to help us in a difficult situation.

During many instances of "taking over" which we have experienced in the war, we have never received such assistance, and that rendered on the most generous scale.

In spite of its magnificent success in the recent fighting, the 1st American Division must have been feeling the strain of the operations accentuated by heavy casualties, yet, we could discern no symptoms of fatigue when it came to a question of adding to it by making our task easier.

To your Artillery Commander (Colonel Holbrook) and his staff and to the units under his command, our special thanks are due. Without hesitation when you saw our awkward predicament as regards artillery support, the guns of your Division denied themselves relief in order to assist us in an attack. This attack was only partly successful but the artillery support was entirely so.

Without the help of Colonel Mabee and his establishment of ambulance cars I have no hesitation in saying that at least 400 of our wounded would still be on our hands in this area.

The 15th (Scottish) Division desires me to say that our hope is that we may have opportunity of rendering some slight return to the 1st American Division for all the latter has done for us, and further that we may yet find ourselves shoulder to shoulder defeating the enemy in what we may hope is the final stage of the war.

H. L. Reed, Major General,
Commanding, 15th (Scottish) Division.

CFDAEF: 26

General Order #38

Headquarters, First Division,

American Expeditionary Forces.

France, July 25, 1918.

The Commanding General wishes to express to the officers and soldiers of this Division his pride in their splendid achievements during the operations of July 18-23. Your magnificent courage and unfaltering fortitude have not only won for you individually the admiration of the Allied Armies, but have written a glorious page in the history of that great country which you represent.

For five long days you have maintained a bitter struggle in one of the world's greatest battles and pushed forward in the face of the enemy's most determined resistance. You would not be denied and you have reached the ultimate objective assigned to you in the battle. You have captured for your own share in the fruits of the victory, 3,500 prisoners and 66 cannons. No such brilliant success can be obtained without losses, but the injury which you have inflicted upon the enemy is many times greater, and today your spirit is unshaken, your courage high, and you are, even now, ready to repeat the lesson you have taught the enemy.

The Commanding General is proud to command such a Division and he expresses to you again the deep gratitude he feels for the splendid soldierly qualities you have so gloriously proven in the unquestioned crucible of the battlefield.

By command of Major General Summerall.

Campbell King,
Chief of Staff.

CFDAEF: 27

General Order #143

France, August 28, 1918.

It fills me with pride to record in General Orders a tribute to the service and achievements of the First and Third Corps, comprising the 1st, 2nd, 3rd, 4th, 26th, 28th, 32nd, and 42nd Divisions of the American Expeditionary Forces.

You came to the battlefield at the crucial hour of the Allied cause. For almost four years the most formidable army the world has as yet seen has pressed its invasion of France, and stood threatening its Capital. At no time had that army been more powerful or menacing than when on July 15th, it struck again to destroy in one great battle the brave men opposed to it and enforce its brutal will upon the world and civilization.

Three days later, in conjunction with our Allies, you counter attacked. The Allied Armies gained a brilliant victory that marks the turning point of the war. You did more than give our brave Allies the support to which as a nation our faith was pledged. You proved that our altruism, our pacific spirit, our sense of justice have not blunted our virility and our courage. You have shown that American initiative and energy are as fit for the test of war as for the pursuits of peace. You have justly won the unstinted praise of our Allies and the eternal gratitude of our countrymen.

We have paid for our successes with the lives of many of our brave comrades. We shall cherish their memory always and claim for our history and literature their bravery, achievements and sacrifice.

John J. Pershing,
General, Commander-in-Chief.
Robert C. Davis,
Adjutant General.

CFDAEF: 28

Aisne-Marne Campaign[154]
July 18 – August 6, 1918

The French high command had made plans for a general converging offensive against the Marne salient. Petain issued orders on 12 July for the attack to begin on the 18th, with five French armies—the Tenth, Sixth, Ninth, Fifth, and Fourth placed around the salient. Spearheading the attack were the five divisions of the French XX Corps, including the American 1st and 2d Divisions. Early on 18 July the two American divisions and a French Moroccan division launched the main blow at the northwest base of the salient near Soissons. Enemy frontline troops, taken by surprise, initially gave ground, although resistance stiffened after an Allied penetration of some three miles. Before the 1st and 2d Divisions were relieved they had advanced 6 to 7 miles, made Soissons untenable for the enemy, and captured 6,500 prisoners at a cost of over 10,000 American casualties.

Meanwhile the other French armies in the offensive made important gains, and the German commander ordered a general retreat from the Marne salient. The French Sixth Army, on the right of the Tenth, advanced from the southwest, reaching the Vesle River on 3 August. By 28 July this army included the American 3d, 4th, 28th, and 42d Divisions. The 4th and 42d Divisions were under control of the I Corps, the first American corps headquarters to participate in combat. On 4 August the American III Corps headquarters entered combat, taking control of the 28th and 32d Divisions. By 5 August the entire Sixth Army front was held by the two American corps. East of the Sixth Army the French Ninth and Fifth Armies also advanced into the salient. The Germans retired across the Aisne and Vesle Rivers, resolutely defending each strong point as they went.

By 6 August the Aisne-Marne Offensive was over. The threat to Paris was ended. The initiative now had passed to the Allies, ending any possibility that Ludendorff could carry out his planned offensive in Flanders. The success of the offensive revealed the advantages of Allied unity of command and the fighting qualities of American units. The eight A.E.F. divisions (1st, 2d, 3d, 4th, 26th, 28th, 32d, 42d) had spearheaded much of the advance, demonstrating offensive capabilities that helped to inspire new confidence in the war-weary Allied armies. About 270,000 Americans took part in the battle.

Soldiers of the 1st Division were awarded the Victory Medal for participation in the Aisne-Marne Campaign

Figure 27: U.S. Army History of the Aisne-Marne Campaign

St. Mihiel Drive

General Order #6

Headquarters,
Fourth Army Corps.
September 13, 1918.

The Fourth Corps has defeated the enemy and driven him back on the whole Corps front. All objectives were reached ahead of the time prescribed, a large number of prisoners and a considerable amount of booty captured. The rapid advance of the Corps, in conjunction with the action of the elements of the First Army, rendered the St. Mihiel salient untenable to the enemy, who has retreated.

The greatest obstacle to the advance was thought to be the enemy's wire, which presented a problem that caused anxiety to all concerned. The Corps Commander desires to express in particular his admiration of the skill shown by the small groups in the advance battalions and their commanders in crossing the hostile wire, and, in general, to express his appreciation of the high spirit and daring shown by the troops, and the rapidity and efficiency with which the operation was conducted.

By command of Major General Dickman.

Steward Heintzelman, Colonel,
General Staff, Chief of Staff.

CFDAEF: 33

Tribute from President Woodrow Wilson

Washington, September 14, 1918.

General John J. Pershing,

American Expeditionary Forces. France.

Accept my warmest congratulations on the brilliant achievements of the Army under your command. The boys have done what we expected of them and done it in the way we most admire. We are deeply proud of them and of their chief. Please convey to all concerned my grateful and affectionate thanks.

CFDAEF: 33

Tribute from the British General Haig

September 14, 1918.

General Pershing, Headquarters,

American Expeditionary Forces. France.

All ranks of the British Armies in France welcome with unbounded admiration and pleasure the victory which has attended the initial offensive of the great American Army under your personal command. I beg you to accept and convey to all ranks my best congratulations and those of all ranks of the British Armies under my command.

CFDAEF: 34

Tribute from General Foch

France, September 14, 1918.
General John J. Pershing,
American Expeditionary Forces. France.

My dear General, the First American Army, under your command on the first day, has won a magnificent victory by a maneuver as skillfully prepared as it was valiantly acted. I extend to you, as well as to the officers and troops under your command, my warmest compliments.

CFDAEF: 34

General Order #56

Headquarters, First Division,
American Expeditionary Forces.
France, September 16, 1918.

The Division Commander desires to express to the officers and men of the Division his appreciation of their gallant conduct in the recent operation against St. Mihiel salient. In spite of formidable wire entanglements, badly broken terrain and most unfavorable weather, the Division went straight to its objectives on schedule time, speedily overcoming the enemy and driving him back in disorder from his strongly organized positions, capturing many prisoners and much valuable war material. Owing to your skill and courage your own losses have been light and you are today stronger and better prepared than ever to administer another blow to the enemy.

As at Soissons, so at St. Mihiel you have gallantly lived up to the best traditions of American manhood and have added another glorious page to the history of our country. The honor of commanding such a division must ever fill with pride the heart of its commander who can confidently look to it to maintain on future battle-fields the splendid record of the past.

C.P. Summerall,
Major General U.S.A.

CFDAEF: 34

General Order #238

France, December 26, 1918.

It is with soldierly pride that I record in General Orders a tribute to the taking of the St. Mihiel salient by the First Army.

On September 12, 1918, you delivered the first concerted offensive operation of the American Expeditionary Forces upon difficult terrain against this redoubtable position, immovably held for 4 years, which crumbled before your able executed advance. Within 24 hours after the commencement of the attack the salient had ceased to exist and you were threatening Metz.

Your divisions, which had never been tried in the exacting conditions of major offensive operations, worthily emulated those of more arduous experience and earned their right to participate in the more difficult task to come. Your staff and auxiliary services, which labored so untiringly and so enthusiastically, deserve equal commendation, and we are indebted to the willing cooperation of veteran French divisions and of auxiliary units which the Allied commands put at our disposal.

Not only did you straighten a dangerous salient, captured 16,000 prisoners and 443 guns and liberated 240 square miles of French territory, but you demonstrated the fitness for battle of a unified American Army.

We appreciate the loyal training and effort of the First Army. In the name of our country, I offer our hearty and unmeasured thanks to these splendid Americans of the 1st, 4th and 5th Corps and of the 1st, 2nd, 4th, 5th, 26th, 42nd, 82nd, 89th, and 90th Divisions, which were engaged, and of the 3rd, 35th, 78th, 80th and 91st Divisions, which were in reserve.

John J. Pershing,
General, Commander-in-Chief.

CFDAEF: 35

St. Mihiel Campaign[155]
September 12 – 16, 1918

By September 1918 there remained one major threat to lateral rail communications behind the Allied lines—the St. Mihiel salient near the Paris-Nancy line. Active preparations for its reduction began with the transfer of Headquarters First Army from La Ferté-sous-Jouarre in the Marne region to Neufchateau on the Meuse, immediately south of St. Mihiel. Because of an earlier priority given to shipment of infantry, the First Army was short of artillery, tank, air, and other support units essential to a well-balanced field army. The French made up this deficiency by loaning Pershing over half the artillery and nearly half the airplanes and tanks needed for the St. Mihiel operation.

The St. Mihiel offensive began on 12 September with a threefold assault on the salient. Total Allied forces involved in the offensive numbered more than 650,000—some 550,000 American and 100,000 Allied troops. In support of the attack the First Army had over 3,000 guns, 400 French tanks, and 1,500 airplanes. Col. William Mitchell directed the heterogeneous air force composed of British, French, Italian, Portuguese, and American units in what proved to be the largest single air operation of the war. American squadrons flew 609 of the airplanes, which were mostly of French or British manufacture.

Defending the salient was German "Army Detachment C," consisting of eight divisions and a brigade in the line and about two divisions in reserve. The Germans had begun a step-by-step withdrawal from the salient only the day before the offensive began. The attack went so well on 12 September that Pershing ordered a speedup in the offensive. By the morning of 13 September the 1st Division joined hands with the 26th Division and before evening all objectives in the salient had been captured. At this point Pershing halted further advances so that American units could be withdrawn for the coming offensive in the Meuse-Argonne sector.

This first major operation by an American Army under its own command[156] took 16,000 prisoners at a cost of 7,000 casualties, eliminated the threat of an attack on the rear of Allied fortifications at Nancy and Verdun, greatly improved Allied lateral rail communications, and opened the way for a possible future offensive to seize Metz and the Briey iron fields.

Soldiers of the 1st Division were awarded the Victory Medal for participation in the St. Mihiel Campaign

Figure 28: U.S. Army History of the St. Mihiel Campaign

Meuse-Argonne Operation

General Order #20

Headquarters First Army,

American Expeditionary Forces.

September 28, 1918.

The Allied troops are now engaged all along the Western Front in the largest combined movement of the war. It is of extreme importance that the 1st American Army drives forward with all possible force.

There is evidence that the enemy is retiring from our own front.

Our success must be followed up with the utmost energy, and pursuit continued to bring about the confusion and demoralization, and to prevent the enemy from forming his shattered forces. I am counting on the splendid spirit, dash and courage of our Army to overcome all opposition. Our country expects nothing else.

John J. Pershing,

General, Commanding First Army.

CFDAEF: 36

Commendation

Advanced Headquarters,

First Army Corps.

October 7, 1918.

From: Chief of Staff, 1st Army Corps, U.S.

To: Commanding General, 1st Division.

Subject: Commendation.

The Corps commander directs me to inform you that the work accomplished by your command has come up to the highest expectations and is up to the standard which has long ago been set and always maintained by the Pioneer Division of the American Expeditionary Forces.

By Command of Major General Liggett.

Malin Craig, Chief of Staff.

CFDAEF: 36

General Order #66

Headquarters, First Division,
American Expeditionary Forces.
France, October 11, 1918.

Pursuant to the orders of the Commander-in-Chief, the undersigned relinquishes command of the 1st Division to assume command of the 5th Army Corps.

It is with the feelings of the most profound regret and with a sense of great personal loss that the honor which has come to me in the command of this Division must be interrupted for service in other fields of usefulness. To the officers and enlisted men of the First Division, I extend the most profound gratitude for the loyalty and devotion with which they have answered every call to duty during the great campaigns in which we have participated together. Throughout its service the 1st Division has served as a model not only to the troops of our own land but to the Armies of the world. They have met and defeated the flower of the great Prussian Army, and in every case where duty has called them they have shown themselves worthy of the finest traditions of our great country and of the armies that have made its history brilliant. The history of the 1st Division will form one of the most brilliant pages in the annals of our nation, and through all generations to come those who formed part of it will associate with pride their participation in its campaigns, and the highest honor that their posterity can enjoy will be that of having an ancestor who shared in the glory of its campaigns.

I have a feeling of certainty that the traditions of this Division will be preserved by those who come after us and that its future will bring even greater victories than those that have distinguished its past. My interest will be continuous and it will be my earnest and constant hope that its successes will contribute in the future as they have in the past to the restoration of the world-peace, and to the maintenance of the lofty ideals for which our country has entered the war.

C.P. Summerall,
Major General, U.S.A., Commanding.
CFDAEF: 37

General Order #201

France, November 19, 1918.

The Commander-in-Chief desires to make record in the General Orders of the American Expeditionary Forces his extreme satisfaction with the conduct of the officers and men of the 1st Division in its advance west of the Meuse between October 4th and 11th, 1918. During this period the Division gained a distance of 7 kilometers over a country which presented not only remarkable facilities for enemy defense, but also great difficulties of terrain for the operations of our troops.

The Division met with resistance from elements of eight hostile divisions, most of which were first class troops and some of which were completely rested. The enemy chose to defend his position to death, and the fighting was always of the most desperate kind. Throughout the operations the officers and men of the Division displayed the highest type of courage, fortitude and self-sacrificing devotion to duty. In addition to many enemy killed, the Division captured 1,407 of the enemy, thirteen 77 mm field guns, 10 trench mortars and numerous machine guns and stores.

The success of the Division in driving a deep advance into the enemy's territory enabled an assault to be made on the left by the neighboring division against the northeastern portion of the Forest of Argonne and enabled the 1st Division to advance to the right and outflank the enemy's position in front of the division on that flank.

The Commander-in-Chief has noted in this Division a special pride of service and a high state of morale, never broken by hardship nor battle.

Official:	By command of General Pershing.
Robert C. Davis,	James W. McAndrew,
Adjutant General.	Chief of Staff. CFDAEF: 41

General Order #232

France, December 19, 1918.

It is with a sense of gratitude for its splendid accomplishments which will live through all history, that I record in General Orders a tribute to the victory of the First Army in the Meuse-Argonne battle.

Tested and strengthened by the reduction of the St. Mihiel salient, for more than six weeks you battered against the pivot of the enemy line on the Western Front. It was a position of imposing natural strength stretching on both sides of the Meuse River from the bitterly contested hills of Verdun to the almost impenetrable forest of the Argonne; a position, moreover, fortified by four years of labor designed to render it impregnable; a position held with the fullest resources of the enemy. That position you broke utterly and thereby hastened the collapse of the enemy's military power.

Soldiers of all the divisions engaged under the 1st, 3rd and 5th American Corps and the 2nd Colonial and 17th French Corps, the 1st, 2nd, 3rd, 4th, 5th, 26th, 28th, 29th, 32nd, 33rd, 35th, 37th, 42nd, 77th, 78th, 79th, 80th, 81st, 82nd, 89th, 90th and 91st American Divisions, the 18th and 26th French Divisions and the 10th and 15th Colonial Divisions—you will be long remembered for the stubborn persistence of your progress, your storming of obstinately defended machine gun nests, your penetration yard by yard of woods and ravines, your heroic resistance in the face of counter-attacks supported by powerful artillery fire. For more than a month, from the initial attack of September 26th, you fought your way slowly through the Argonne, through the woods and over hills west of the Meuse; you slowly enlarged your hold on the Côtes de Meuse on the east, and then, on the 1st of November, your attack forced the enemy into flight. Pressing his retreat you cleared the entire left bank of the Meuse south of Sedan, and then stormed the heights on the right bank and drove him into the plain beyond.

Soldiers of all Army and Corps troops engaged: to you no less credit is due; your steadfast adherence to duty and your dogged determination in the face of all obstacles made possible the heroic deeds cited above.

The achievement of the 1st Army, which is scarcely to be equaled in American history, must remain a source of proud satisfaction to the troops who participated in the last campaign of the war. The American people will remember it as a realization of the hitherto potential strength of the American contribution to the cause to which they had sworn allegiance. There can be no greater reward for a soldier or for a soldier's memory.

Official	John J. Pershing,
Robert C. Davis,	General, Commander-in-Chief,
Adjutant General. ·	American Expeditionary Forces.

CFDAEF: 42

Sedan

General Order #26

France, November 20, 1918.

The following citations are announced:

The 1st, 2nd and 89th Divisions, 5th Corps, American E.F., for their part in the memorable attack launched by the 1st American Army on the 1st of November. Throughout this operation all officers and men, by their high courage, devotion to duty and disregard for the innumerable hardships encountered, made themselves a place in the history of our country.

Extract.

"The 1st Division, American E.F., (Brig. General Frank Parker, Commanding), extended the left of the Corps during the advance, after a long and hard march, took up the pursuit of the enemy, marching, fighting day and night with great courage and determination. It added to its already brilliant record by an historical march of two days and nights, arriving on the heights southeast of the city of Sedan."

Official:	C.P. Summerall,
Harry C. Kaefring,	Major General, Commanding.
Adjutant General.	

CFDAEF: 41

Commendation

Headquarters, Fifth Army Corps,

American Expeditionary Forces.

France, November 10, 1918.

From: Commanding General, 5th Army Corps.

To: Commanding General, 1st Division.

Upon the relief of the 1st Division from service with the 5th Army Corps, I desire to convey to you and to the officers and soldiers of the Division my profound appreciation of the high standards of the maneuvering and fighting power that exists in the Division, and of the energetic and able manner in which the Division responds to every task entrusted to it.

The 1st Division was relieved from this Corps on October 10th after a prolonged and desperate battle in which it suffered unusually heavy casualties. It returned to the rear area, was recruited and trained and was again able to take its place in the lines as a first class combat division on October 30th. As Corps Reserve it followed the operation of this Corps during the advance commenced November 1st, and was placed in line for assault on November 5. The records show that within 48 hours it marched all night for two nights, fought all day for two days and covered at least 60 kilometers across country and through woods, and for the last 10 kilometers in the face of the enemy. By its vigorous and powerful action it drove the enemy across the river as far as Mouzon and made a dash to the hills south of Sedan where it formed preparatory to an assault on the place.

The country may well feel proud of such an organization and all officers and soldiers of the 1st Division may justly cherish the privilege serving with it during this period of the war.

C. P. Summerall,

Major General, Commanding.

CFDAEF: 40

General Order #203

France, November 12, 1918.

The enemy has capitulated. It is fitting that I address myself with thanks directed to the officers and men of the American Expeditionary Forces, who by their heroic efforts, have made possible this glorious result. Our armies, hurriedly and hastily trained, met a veteran enemy, and by courage, discipline and skill always defeated him. Without complaint you have endured incessant toil, privation and danger. You have seen many of your comrades make the supreme sacrifice that freedom may live. I thank you for the patience and courage with which you have endured. I congratulate you upon the splendid fruits of victory which your heroism and the blood of our gallant dead are now presenting to our nation. Your deeds will live forever on the most glorious pages of America's history.

Those things you have done. There remains now a harder task which will test your soldiery qualities to the utmost. Succeed in this and little note will be taken and few praises will be sung; fail, and the light of your glorious achievements of the past will sadly be dimmed. But you will not fail. Every natural tendency may urge towards relaxation in discipline, in conduct, in appearance, in everything that marks the soldier. Yet you will remember that each officer and each soldier is the representative in Europe of his people and that his brilliant deeds of yesterday permit no action of today to pass unnoticed by friend or foe. You will meet this test as gallantly as you have met the tests of the battlefield. Sustained by your high ideals and inspired by the heroic part you have played, you will carry back to your people the proud consciousness of a new Americanism of sacrifice.

Whether you stand on hostile territory or on the friendly soil of France, you will so bear yourselves in discipline, appearance and respect for civil rights that you will confirm for all time the pride and love which every American feels for your uniform and for you.

Official: John J. Pershing,
Robert C. Davis,   General, Commander-in-Chief.
Adjutant General.

CFDAEF: 44

General Order #204

France, November 12, 1918.

The following proclamation from the Commander-in-Chief of the Allied Armies is published to the Command:

*****

G.H.Q., November 12, 1918.

Officers, Non-Commissioned Officers, Soldiers of the Allied Armies:

After having resolutely stopped the enemy, you have continuously attacked him for months with a confidence and an energy that never slackened.

You have won the greatest battle of history, and saved the most sacred cause—the Liberty of the World.

Be proud of the immortal glory with which you have crowned your flags.

Posterity keeps for you her gratitude.

F. Foch,
Marshal of France,
Commander-in-Chief of the Allied Armies.

CFDAEF: 45

Meuse-Argonne Campaign[157]
September 26 – November 11, 1918

The objective of the campaign was to drive the enemy out of France before winter and end the war in the spring of 1919. The fall offensive, designed to prevent a step-by-step enemy retirement, called for a gigantic pincers movement with the objective of capturing Aulnoye and Mézières. The British army was assigned the task of driving toward Aulnoye, while the A.E.F. was designated for the southern arm of the pincers, the thrust on Mézières. Simultaneously the Belgian-French-British army group in Flanders would drive toward Ghent, and the French armies in the Oise-Aisne region would exert pressure all along their front to lend support to the pincers attack. Pershing decided to strike his heaviest blow in a zone about 20 miles wide between the Heights of the Meuse on the east and the Argonne Forest on the west. The task of assembling troops in the concentration area between Verdun and the Argonne was complicated by the fact that many American units were currently engaged in the St. Mihiel battle. Some 600,000 Americans had to be moved into the Argonne sector while 220,000 French moved out.

The Meuse-Argonne Offensive was in three phases. During the first phase (September 26 – October 3) the First Army advanced through most of the southern Meuse-Argonne region, captured enemy strong points, seized the first two German defense lines, and then stalled before the third line. Failure of tank support, a difficult supply situation, and the inexperience of American troops all contributed to checking its advance. In the second phase (October 4 - 31) the First Army, after the inexperienced divisions had been replaced by veteran units, slowly ground its way through the third German line. By the end of October the enemy had been cleared from the Argonne and First Army troops were through the German main positions. Before the third phase (November 1-11), many of the exhausted divisions of the First Army were replaced, roads were built or repaired, supply was improved, and most Allied units serving with the A.E.F. were withdrawn. On November 1 First Army units began the assault of the now strengthened German fourth line of defense.

General Pershing authorized the results of the Meuse-Argonne Campaign, the greatest battle in American history up to that time, published in his Final

Report: "Between September 26 and November 11, 22 American and 4 French divisions, on the front extending from southeast of Verdun to the Argonne Forest, had engaged and decisively beaten 47 different German divisions.... The First Army suffered a loss of about 117,000 in killed and wounded. It captured 26,000 prisoners, 847 cannons, 3,000 machine guns, and large quantities of material."

More than 1,200,000 Americans had taken part in the 47-day campaign.

Soldiers of the 1st Division were awarded the Victory Medal for participation in the Meuse-Argonne Campaign.

Figure 29: U.S. Army History of the Meuse-Argonne Campaign

REGISTER OF NOTES

1   Armistice is the end of hostilities by mutual agreement between the belligerent   xii
parties.

2   Lieutenant Colonel John McCrae was a Canadian physician serving in the Canadian   xii
Army. "In Flanders Fields" was published in *Punch* magazine on December 8, 1915.

3   The dates in the diary and memoirs recognizing the appointment of Charles Edward   xvi
Dilkes as acting sergeant (January 18, 1918) and promotion to rank of sergeant (April
2, 1918) occur later than the dates recorded in the Enlistment Record (July 23, 1917).

4   Wartime rank was reduced to peacetime rank once the Armistice was signed (ref.   xvi
Coffman, E.M., p. 359).

5   Military service record of Charles Edward Dilkes as recorded by the Society of the   xvii
First Division.

6   "Map of Europe 1914." History Department atlases index. United States Military   xviii
Academy. 28 April 2007 <http://www.dean.usma.edu/history/web03/atlases/index.
htm>.

7   "After Blenheim" was written by Robert Southey in 1798 and published in *The Golden*   xx
Treasury of Songs and Lyrics by Francis T. Palgrave, The MacMillan Company, NYC,
NY, 1928. It is a poem about the lasting effects of the Battle of Blenheim and the
victory of the Duke of Marlborough over Prince Eugene, who helped establish the
Austrian-Hungarian Empire.

8   Austria-Hungary was a member of the Central Powers who opposed the Allied Armies   xxiii
in World War I. The geographic integrity of Austria-Hungary was dissolved as a result
of the peace treaty that ended World War I.

9   Teutonic refers to a tall blond race characteristic of northern Europe with a military   xxiii
history of winning power and prestige.

10   Western Front was the armed frontier defined by the German border with Germany   xxiii
to the east and the Allied Armies to the west; it was marked by a line of trenches
that ran from the coast of northern France and Belgium to France's border with
Switzerland.

11   "Forty years of preparedness" refers to the rise of the German Empire, in particular   xxiii
Germany's success in the Franco-Prussian War in 1871, which resulted in Germany
undermining the dominance of France in Europe.

12   Imperial Castle refers to a symbol of the German Nation.   xxiii

13   As documented in the United States Army Center of Military History (1998). "The   xxiv
World War to May 28, 1918, and the Organization of the American Expeditionary
Forces," *United States Army in World War I*, version 2, CD-ROM disc 3 of 3: 11.

14   McMurry, Frank M. *The Geography of the Great War.* MacMillan Co., NY, 1919.   2
Figure 17 - Page 20. 28 April 2007 <http://freepages.military.rootsweb.ancestry.
com/~worldwarone/WWI/>.

15   Despite the secrecy imposed on activities leading up to the troops' departure, most   4
likely a crowd of people had waited outside the gates to the Washington Barracks in
anticipation of the departure.

16   The *SS Finland* was an American passenger steamship built in 1902 and placed into   4
service by the US Army in 1917 to transport US troops to Europe to participate in the
war. In 1918 the ship was transferred to the US Navy and commissioned as the *USS
Finland*.

17   Crow's nest is a box or perch near the top of the ship's mast used by the person on   5
lookout.

18   Semaphore is a system of communication by signaling with the use of two flags.   6

19   *A History of the 1st U.S. Engineers - 1st U.S. Division* references the *Finland's* arrival   7
on the 20th and the landing of the engineers on the 21st of August, 1917.

20   United States Army Center of Military History (1998). "Order of Battle of the United   8
States Land Forces in the World War, American Expeditionary Forces: Divisions,"
United States Army in World War I, version 2, CD-ROM disc 3 of 3, (volume II) 5+.

21   A major obstacle to America's entry into the war was how to transport her troops   9
from America to Europe. The number of ships allocated from our Allies was less
than needed. America's resourcefulness in troop transport paved the way for a
successful entry.

22   Trains were used to transport troops from their port of embarkation to their point of   10
service in the war. "Railway Routes...A.E.F. France." Office of Medical History. U.S.
Army Medical Department. 28 April 2007 <http://history.amedd.army.mil/booksdocs/
wwi/fieldoperations/ch7plt1.pdf>.

23   Ed: A class society existed at this time in American history; this class society was   11
depicted in movies such as the 1997 film <u>Titanic</u>. The Dilkes family was a member of
Philadelphia society.

24   "*40 hommes, 8 chevaux*" is French for "40 men, 8 horses."   12

25   Barbed wire is wire with sharp points all along it, which is commonly used for   12
military defenses and for safely securing animals.

26   Ed: The events that occurred while on guard duty may not necessarily have occurred   12
on the same watch.

27   Cantonment is the living quarters assigned to a body of troops.   12

28   *Curé* is a French priest.   12

29   Liquid fire is an incendiary weapon such as a flamethrower used by both sides in the   13
world conflict.

30   United States Army Center of Military History (1998). "Training and Use of American   14
Units with the British and French," *United States Army in World War I*, version 2, CD-
ROM disc 1 of 3 (volume III) 449.

31   The map of the Lunéville-Sommerviller Sector is found in the United States Center of   16
Military History (1998). "American Armies and Battlefields in Europe," *United States
Army in World War I*, version 2, CD-ROM disc 3 of 3: 422.

32   Ed: The *Antilles* was an American transport ship that was sunk by a German   17
submarine on October 17, 1917; 67 lives were lost.

33   Ed: In a separate incident, the date November 3, 1917, is remembered as the day   18
the first Americans were killed on the soil of France. ACKNOWLEDGEMENT FROM
GENERAL BORDEAUX–"The death of this humble corporal and these privates
appeals to us with unwonted grandeur. We will, therefore, ask that the mortal remains
of these young men be left here, be left to us forever. We will inscribe on their
tombs, 'here lie the first soldiers of the United States to fall on the fields of France for
justice and liberty.' The passer-by will stop and uncover his head. The travelers of
France, of the Allied countries, of America, the men of heart, who will come to visit
our battlefields of Lorraine, will go out of their way to come here to bring to these
graves the tribute of their respect and gratitude. Corporal Gresham, Private Enright
and Private Hay, in the name of France, I thank you." Recorded in the original
Commendations of First Division American Expeditionary Forces (CFDAEF): 8.

34   Parapet is an elevated wall of earth built for the protection of a soldier.   18

35   The whole battle front is the battle line in the Vosges Mountain region. The 1st   18
Division engineers operated in the Lunéville and Sommerviller sectors in the Vosges
region.

36   Strasbourg/Strassburg has been a contested city over the centuries between France   18
and Germany. The French spelling is Strasbourg (map p. 14); the German spelling
is Strassburg (map p. xxvi). On November 4, 1917, the city was under German
jurisdiction.

37	Ed: J.A.D. is Charles Edward Dilkes' brother, James Alphonsus Dilkes.	20
38	Paul Fussell in his book *The Great War and Modern Memory* in the chapter on "Myth, Ritual, and Romance" referred to such purported spy activities as rumors that originated in the Great War and were propagated in succeeding wars, p. 120.	20
39	The Rainbow Division (42nd Division) was formed in 1917 as one combat unit from National Guard regiments and units from 26 States and the District of Columbia. The first chief of staff was then Colonel Douglas MacArthur who commented that "the division stretches across America like a rainbow."	20
40	*The Double Traitor* was written in 1915 by E. Phillips Oppenheim.	21
41	Klaxon horn was a hand-powered horn made by an English company, Klaxon Signals Ltd., and typically used to alert possible danger.	21
42	Propergander is a colloquialism for propaganda, which is designed to propagate world views that are consistent with the issuer's stance. The most common format for propergander in WWI was printed material, especially posters and leaflets.	21
43	Kilometer is a measure of length equivalent to five-eighths of a mile.	21
44	"First Division Ansauville Sector January 15 - April 3, 1918." Office of Medical History. U.S. Army Medical Department. 28 April 2007. <http://history.amedd.army.mil/booksdocs/wwi/fieldoperations/ch9plt2.pdf>.	22
45	Camp Essayons is located on "Battle Maps–Charts–Sketches" at the National Archives in College Park, MD. Record Group 120.	23
46	To be billeted in barracks is to be assigned living quarters.	24
47	No-man's-land is the land between the trenches of opposing forces.	25
48	Hun was the term used in reference to the German army when viewed as ruthless and barbaric.	25
49	*Kamerad* is the German word for comrade or friend.	25
50	One trick used by German soldiers was to give the allusion they wanted to surrender while their comrades prepared to slaughter Allied troops.	25
51	United States Army Center of Military History (1998). "Training and Use of American Units with the British and French," *United States Army in World War I*, version 2, CD-ROM disc 1 of 3 (volume III) 464.	26
52	The Allied Armies were represented by up to 38 countries. The main members were France, Great Britain, Russia, Italy, and the United States (map p. xvi).	27
53	Military history documents ten prisoners were captured during the Division's tour in the Ansauville sector. Commendations of the First Division American Expeditionary Forces 1917 - 1919 France * Germany : 15.	27
54	The German aviator was observing the Allied position for military intelligence.	28
55	Shrapnel is a piece of metal that splits off from an exploding artillery or mortar round; shell fragment.	28
56	Cannonading is the firing of cannons and other heavy artillery.	28
57	Aeroplane is the early twentieth century spelling of airplane.	28
58	Doughboy is an American infantry man or foot soldier.	29
59	Mustard gas is a poison gas, with an odor like ground mustard, used in warfare because of its irritating, blistering, and debilitating effects.	30
60	Double-quick timed (double time, double-quick step) is the fastest time in marching next to the run.	30
61	United States Army Center of Military History (1998). "Training and Use of American Units with the British and French," *United States Army in World War I*, version 2, CD-ROM disc 1 of 3 (volume III) 487.	32
62	A.W.O.L. is Absent With Out Leave.	33
63	On April 2 Charles Edward Dilkes was promoted from acting sergeant to sergeant.	34

64	*Hic, haec, hoc* used here is a spoof on the Latin declension of the demonstrative pronoun "this." Formally it is the Latin singular of "this" and is written here in order of gender: masculine, feminine, neuter.	35
65	Military histories refer to the Algerians as part of the French Colonial Army. James Carl Nelson, author, mentioned the Algerians in Cantigny and Soissons (Aisne-Marne).	35
66	Boche is a derogatory name for a German soldier.	36
67	Sous is a form of French currency equivalent at the time to a half-penny.	38
68	*Vin rouge (vinny rouge)* is French for red wine.	40
69	Corporal of the Guard is a sentinel watch.	40
70	A mule skinner is a driver of the mule-driven supply wagons.	40
71	Varmaise, a town that virtually disappeared, was the site of the engineers' aid station. *A History of the 1st U.S. Engineers:* 20.	42
72	Commendations of First Division American Expeditionary Forces 1917 – 1919 France * Germany: 15.	43
73	United States Center of Military History (1998). "American Armies and Battlefields in Europe," *United States Army in World War I,* version 2, CD-ROM disc 3 of 3: 415.	44
74	United States Army Center of Military History (1998). "Military Operations of the American Expeditionary Forces," *United States Army in World War I,* version 2, CD-ROM disc 1 of 3 (volume IV) 272.	48
75	The French referred to the German soldier as Fritz.	49
76	Troops of the 1st Division were trained by the French and fought under French command at this point in the war.	50
77	*Capt. Cinquante Cinq* is artillery that shoots a 155 mm shell—a little more than six inches in diameter.	56
78	The Blue Devils were an elite fighting unit of the French Army.	60
79	The American soldier referred to the German soldier as a Dutchman (Deutschman).	60
80	Engineers were cited for their work under heavy bombardment and yet completed on schedule. *A History of the 1st U.S. Engineers*: 21.	60
81	Fusillade is the simultaneous discharge of many firearms.	61
82	To take to the top is to get out of the trenches and walk along the top of the trench.	61
83	United States Army Center of Military History (1998). "Policy-forming Documents of the American Expeditionary Forces," *United States Army in World War I,* version 2, CD-ROM disc 1 of 3 (volume II) 434.	63
84	Golden rain refers to the chemical warfare and gas attacks.	64
85	*Vin blanc* is French for white wine.	67
86	Annette Kellerman was a swimming sensation who adapted her swimming prowess for vaudeville and was known as the Diving Venus.	69
87	NCO is a non-commissioned officer.	69
88	The Cantigny operation had merged into the Montdidier-Noyon Campaign.	70
89	A young barrage is an impromptu, newly formed barrage.	71
90	"World War I Victory Medal." The Institute of Heraldry. Office of the Administrative Assistant to the Secretary of the Army. 01 January 2014 < http://www.tioh.hqda. pentagon.mil/Catalog/Heraldry.aspx?HeraldryId=15283&CategoryId=4&grp=4&menu =Decorations and Medals&ps=24&p=0&hilite=Victory Medal>	73
91	"Aisne-Marne Operation (Soissons) First Division July 17 - 23, 1918." Office of Medical History. U.S. Army Medical Department. 28 April 2007. <http://history. amedd.army.mil/booksdocs/wwi/fieldoperations/ch12plt6.pdf>.	74

92	Included in Commendations of First Division American Expeditionary Forces 1917 – 1919 France * Germany: 28 - 29.	78
93	Named the International Committee of the Red Cross in 1876, the society was founded to relieve suffering in time of war. The Red Cross provided relief during World War I.	80
94	Gerry is a British term for a German soldier.	83
95	Blighty is a British term for a wound.	83
96	Gordon Highlanders are an elite fighting unit of the British Army - Scottish Division.	84
97	The Signal Corps is a branch of the U.S. Army responsible for military communications.	84
98	MP is military police.	86
99	Hummer means a time noted for great energy, spirit, activity, or liveliness.	87
100	General Ferdinand Foch was Chief of French General Staff when the U.S. entered the War. He was made General of the Allied Forces on the Western Front, subsequently promoted to Field Marshall and served as the Supreme Allied Commander.	88
101	The plan of attack for the St. Mihiel campaign is referenced on the web site: <http://www.worldwar1.com/maps/usa523.jpg>.	90
102	Delousing is the action used to exterminate lice.	91
103	Cooties are lice.	91
104	A bangalore is a metal tube filled with high explosives used to blast a path through barbed wire entanglements.	91
105	United States Army Center of Military History (1998). "Military Operations of the American Expeditionary Forces," *United States Army in World War I*, version 2, CD-ROM Disc 1 of 3 (volume IX) 79.	94
106	Squad column is a common military formation for maneuverability where one component is placed behind another component.	96
107	"St. Mihiel 1st Division." Office of Medical History. U.S. Army Medical Department. 28 April 2007. <http://history.amedd.army.mil/booksdocs/wwi/fieldoperations/ch16plt22.pdf>.	97
108	The Iron Cross was originally established by King Friedrich Wilhelm III in March, 1813. On August 5, 1914, Wilhelm II, Emperor of Germany and the King of Prussia, reestablished the medal. The Iron Cross was awarded without regard for nationality or social class to combatants for acts of heroism, bravery, or leadership skills. During the First World War Germany awarded over five million of these medals to members of the armed forces: Grand Cross (5), First Class (288,000) and Second Class (5,200,000).	98
109	Hard-tack is a hard biscuit usually baked in large round cakes without salt.	100
110	United States Army Center of Military History (1998). "American Armies and Battlefields in Europe: American Operations in the Meuse-Argonne Region," *United States Army in World War I*, version 2, CD-ROM disc 3 of 3: 226.	102
111	Lt. Col. Frederick Palmer was attached to the Intelligence Section of the General Staff during the War and was probably the best-known war correspondent at the time. He wrote a story in *Collier's Weekly* which contained an account of the battles fought by the First Division in the Meuse-Argonne operation.	105
112	CFDAEF refers to the Commendations of the First Division American Expeditionary Forces.	106
113	United States Army Center of Military History (1998). "American Armies and Battlefields in Europe: American Operations in the Meuse-Argonne Region," *United States Army in World War I*, version 2, CD-ROM disc 3 of 3: 228.	107

114   United States Army Center of Military History (1998). "American Armies and   111
Battlefields in Europe: American Operations in the Meuse-Argonne Region," *United
States Army in World War I*, version 2, CD-ROM disc 3 of 3: 228-230.

115   United States Army Center of Military History (1998). "American Armies and   112
Battlefields in Europe: American Operations in the Meuse-Argonne Region," *United
States Army in World War I*, version 2, CD-ROM disc 3 of 3: 296.

116   Slum is a stew made from a variety of food and canned meat.   113

117   Corn bill is a type of corn-based porridge.   113

118   United States Army Center of Military History (1998). "American Armies and   116
Battlefields in Europe: American Operations in the Meuse-Argonne Region," *United
States Army in World War I*, version 2, CD-ROM disc 3 of 3: 297-298.

119   United States Army Center of Military History (1998). "American Armies and   119
Battlefields in Europe: After the Armistice," *United States Army in World War I*,
version 2, CD-ROM disc 3 of 3: 487.

120   "*La Marseillaise*" is the French national anthem.   120

121   Oelingen can be found on a map in Records of the American Expeditionary Forces   120
1917 - 1921 at the National Archives, College Park, MD, Record Group 120, Series 65.

122   Luxembourg is the spelling for the independent country and also the French   120
spelling. Luxemburg as shown on the maps is the German spelling when the
country was under German jurisdiction.

123   The Salvation Army is an international organization for religious and philanthropic   120
purposes that works within the community.

124   *Herr* German is a German man, typically the head of a household or business.   121

125   United States Army Center of Military History (1998). "Military Operations of the   122
American Expeditionary Forces," *United States Army in World War I*, version 2, CD-
ROM disc 1 of 3 (volume IX) 391-392.

126   United States Army Center of Military History (1998). "American Armies and   124
Battlefields in Europe: After the Armistice," *United States Army in World War I*,
version 2, CD-ROM disc 3 of 3: 489.

127   Pontoon bridge is a temporary bridge supported by floating objects used for the   125
passage of troops.

128   "Yow" is an exclamation of excitement or surprise.   125

129   *Frau* is a German married woman.   125

130   The morale problem in the A.E.F. is well documented in Edward Coffman's book   126
The War to End All Wars: The American Military Experience in World War I, p. 358.

131   Charles Edward Dilkes' comments about the First Division being the first to go to   126
war and the last to come home were also noted in "Strange As It Seems," *Newark
Ledger*, February 8, 1934.

132   The Chicago Historical Society includes a similar rendition of "Darling I Am Coming   127
Back" on their web site. 15 January 2009 <http://ecuip.lib.uchicago.edu/diglib/
social/chi1919/aline/a1/19a1d3.html>.

133   "The Payday Song" appears in *A History of the 1st U.S. Engineers - 1st U.S. Division*   127
:112.

134   Marie-Louise Dilkes was a volunteer representative in Paris for the Emergency Aid of   128
Pennsylvania. She helped establish a canteen for American servicemen, which was
known as the American Soldiers' & Sailors' Club.

135   A.E.F. stands for the American Expeditionary Forces. It was the name given to the   128
American troops serving in Europe in World War I.

136   Prussia was an area of central Europe in WWI that was composed of parts of   128
Germany, Poland, and Russia. It was dissolved after WWI into its component parts.

137   "Strange As It Seems," John Hix, *Newark Ledger*, February 8, 1934.   129

138   In the heat of argument the German would use an invective epithet to rile his   129
American adversary.

139   *Fraulein* is the German word for a girl or unmarried woman.   130

140   Schnapps is the German word for an unsweetened alcoholic beverage.   130

141   A shave-tail is a second lieutenant whose job is to recruit soldiers.   131

142   Y.M.C.A. stands for Young Men's Christian Association.   131

143   "*Quand Même*" is a versatile French expression. *Vive la France, Quand Même!*   133
(Long Live France, Still!) appears on World War I memorials throughout France.
It means "even so" or "all the same" or "anyway." It was the motto for the actress
Sarah Bernhardt and for Marie-Louise Dilkes.

144   United States Army Center of Military History (1998). "American Occupation   135
of Germany," *United States Army in World War I,* version 2, CD-ROM disc 2 of 3
(Volume XI) 144.

145   United States Army Center of Military History (1998). "American Occupation   137
of Germany," *United States Army in World War I,* version 2, CD-ROM disc 2 of 3
(Volume XI) 123.

146   United States Army Center of Military History (1998). "Order of Battle of the United   138
States Land Forces in the World War," *United States Army in World War I*, version 2,
CD-ROM disc 3 of 3, (vol. 3: part 3, Zone of the Interior: Directory of Troops) 337.

147   General Order No. 38-A is a personal thank you from General John J. Pershing for   139
the First Division's service to our nation.

148   Rudyard Kipling (1865-1936) was a British writer who was born in India, educated in   141
England, and returned to India to write. He won the Nobel Prize in literature in 1907.

149   "Map of Europe 1919." History Department atlases index. United States Military   144
Academy. 08 January 2009 <http://www.dean.usma.edu/history/web03/atlases/
index.htm>.

150   Minnenwerfer is a piece of German artillery, typically a mounted gun or cannon   147
commonly used in a rolling barrage.

151   The Great Republic is the United States of America.   147

152   "Montdidier-Noyon, 9 - 13 June 1918." Named Campaigns - World War I. The U.S.   152
Army Center of Military History. 28 March 2011 <http://www.history.army.mil/html/
reference/army_flag/wwi.html>.

153   General John J. Pershing related the Battle for Cantigny in his book, *My Experiences*   152
in the World War, vol. II, p. 59.

154   "Aisne-Marne, 18 July - 6 August 1918." Named Campaigns - World War I. The U.S.   157
Army Center of Military History. 28 April 2007 <http://www.army.mil/cmh-pg/
reference/wicmp.htm>.

155   "St. Mihiel, 12 - 16 September 1918." Named Campaigns - World War I. The U.S. Army   162
Center of Military History. 28 April 2007 <http://www.army.mil/cmh-pg/reference/
wicmp.htm>.

156   General John J. Pershing in his memoirs details his persistence and determination to   162
have American soldiers fight under American command and under their own flag.

157   "Meuse-Argonne, 26 September - 11 November 1918." U.S. Army Campaigns: World   171
War I. The U.S. Army Center of Military History. 06 March 2010 <http://www.history.
army.mil/html/reference/army_flag/wwi.html>.

GLOSSARY

A.E.F.	American Expeditionary Forces—a name given to the American troops serving in Europe in World War I
A.W.O.L.	A personnel who has left his unit without authorization—Absent With Out Leave
Aeroplane	Early twentieth century spelling of airplane
Armistice	End of hostilities and the beginning of discussions for a peace treaty
Bangalore	Metal tube filled with high explosives used to blast a path through barbed wire entanglements
Barbed wire	Wire with many sharp points all along it, which was used for military defenses
Billeted	Assigned living quarters
Blighty	British term for a wound
Blue Devils	Elite fighting unit of the French Army
Boche	Derogatory name for a German soldier
Cannonading	Firing cannons and other heavy artillery
Cantonment	Place assigned to a body of troops for living quarters
Capt. Cinquante-Cinq	Artillery that shoots a 155 mm shell
CFDAEF	A collection of Commendations of the First Division American Expeditionary Forces
Chevaux	French word for horses
Cooties	Lice
Corn bill	Type of corn-based porridge
Corporal of the Guard	Sentinel watch
Crow's nest	Box or perch near the top of the ship's mast used by the person on lookout
Curé	French priest

Delousing	Action used to exterminate lice
Double quick-step	(Double time) The fastest time in marching—next to the run
Double traitor	Spy in the neighborhood
Doughboy	American infantry man or foot soldier
Dutchman / Deutschman	American name for a German soldier
Engineer train	A horsed or motorized train that carried the tools the engineers used and sometimes the engineers, too
Frau	A German married woman
Fraulein	German word for girl or unmarried woman
Fritz	French term for a German soldier
Fusillade	Simultaneous discharge of many firearms
Gerry	British term for a German soldier
Golden rain	Toxic gases
Gordon Highlanders	An elite fighting unit of the British Army
Great Republic	United States of America
Hard-tack	Hard biscuit made of flour and water and usually without salt
Herr German	A German man, typically the head of a household or business
Hic, haec, hoc	Latin singular for the demonstrative pronoun "this" according to gender: masculine, feminine, neuter
Hommes	French word for men
Hummer	A time noted for great energy, spirit, activity or liveliness
Hun	A term used in reference to the German soldier when viewed as ruthless and barbaric
Imperial Castle	Reference to the German Empire; home of Kaiser Wilhelm II
Iron Cross	A German military award for heroism, bravery, or leadership without regard for nationality or social class
Kamerad	German for comrade or friend
Kilometer	Measure of length equivalent to five-eighths of a mile; also referred to as a kilo
Klaxon horn	A hand-powered horn typically used to alert possible danger
Liquid fire	Flaming substance used as an incendiary weapon in warfare typically as a flamethrower
Minnenwerfer	German artillery, typically a mounted gun or cannon designed to hurl large projectiles
MP	Military Police
Mule skinner	Driver of the mule-driven supply wagons
Mustard gas	Poison gas, with an odor like ground mustard, used in warfare because of its irritating, blistering, and debilitating effects
NCO	Non-commissioned officer
No-man's-land	Land between the trenches of the opposing forces

Parapet	An elevated wall of earth built for the protection of the soldier
Pontoon bridge	A temporary bridge supported by floating objects used for the passage of troops
Propaganda / propergander	The scheme for the propagation of information to influence people
Quand même	French for even so; all the same; anyway
Rauchen verboten	German for smoking forbidden
Reconnoiter	To observe one's enemy's strength or position
Salient	The part of a battle line with an outward projection
Schnapps	German word for an unsweetened alcoholic beverage
Semaphore	A system of communication by signaling with the use of two flags
Sentinel watch	A soldier or guard who is assigned to stand and keep watch
Shave-tail	A second lieutenant whose job is to recruit soldiers
Shrapnel	A piece of metal that splits off from an exploding artillery or mortar round; shell fragment
Slum	Stew made from a variety of food and canned meat
Sous	French currency equivalent to a half-penny
Spud	A potato
Squad column	Common military formation for maneuverability where one component is placed behind another component
Take to the top	Get out of the trenches and walk along the top of the trench
Teutonic	A tall blond race characteristic of northern Europe with a military history of winning power and prestige
Vin blanc	French for white wine
Vin rouge (vinny rouge)	French for red wine
Y.M.C.A.	Young Men's Christian Association
Young barrage	An impromptu newly formed wall of fire provided by artillery or machine guns
Yow	An American exclamation of excitement or surprise

BIBLIOGRAPHY

Primary Sources

Combat Division Records of the 1st - 20th Divisions 1917. Entry 1241. Boxes 108 -110. National Archives. College Park, MD.

"Commendations of First Division American Expeditionary Forces 1917 – 1919 France * Germany." G.O. No. 201. G.H.Q., A.E.F., Nov. 19, 1918.

Dilkes, Charles Edward. Original Manuscript of the Diary of Charles Edward Dilkes and his participation in World War I: 1917 – 1919. The Dilkes Family Papers.

Dilkes, Charles Edward. Original Manuscript of the Memoirs of Charles Edward Dilkes and his participation in World War I: 1917 – 1919. The Dilkes Family Papers.

Dilkes, Charles Edward. Letter from Crédit Lyonnais Bank to Sgt. Charles E. Dilkes. 27 April 1918. The Dilkes Family Papers.

Dilkes, Charles Edward. Private Papers of the Years: 1917 - 1919. The Dilkes Family Papers.

Dilkes, Marie-Louise. American Soldiers' and Sailors' Club card. April 1919.

Hix, John. "Strange As It Seems." *The Newark Ledger.* 8 February 1934.

Legge, Barnwell R., Ray, William A., and Ransom, Paul L. "Battle Maps - Charts - Sketches." March 1918. Record Group 120. National Archives. College Park, MD.

Mangin, French General Charles Marie Emmanuel. "General Order 318." 30 July 1918. Original document in the private papers of Charles Edward Dilkes. The Dilkes Family Papers.

Myers, George S. "Photographs of the War." Patrol Dept. Hercules, Calif. U.S.A.

Pershing, General John J. "General Order 38-A: Farewell from General Pershing." 28 February 1919. Original document in the private papers of Charles Edward Dilkes. The Dilkes Family Papers.

Picture of Sgt. Charles Edward Dilkes, France. Personal photograph by unknown photographer. 1918. Private collection of original World War I photographs. The Dilkes Family Collection.

Records of the American Expeditionary Forces 1917 - 1921. Record Group 120, Series 65, National Archives. College Park, MD.

"War Ended 6 A.M. Today; Truce Signed Midnight; Glorious Allied Peace," *Evening Public Ledger and The Evening Telegraph*. Philadelphia, PA. 11 November 1918: 1.

Secondary Sources

"1st Division (RA) Record of Events." U.S. Army Center of Military History. 15 January 2009. <http://www.history.army.mil/books/wwi/ob/1-ROE-OB.htm>.

"Aisne-Marne Campaign." Map. Based on the map illustrated on the Medical Department of the United States Army in the World War website: Plate VI. 04 June 2009. <http://history.amedd.army.mil/booksdocs/wwi/fieldoperations/default.htm>.

"Ansauville Sector." Map. Based on the map illustrated on the Medical Department of the United States Army in the World War website: Plate II. 04 June 2009. <http://history.amedd.army.mil/booksdocs/wwi/fieldoperations/default.htm>.

Armistice and the German Army Retreating. Map. Based on the map illustrated in the United States Army of Military History (2001). "American Armies and Battlefields in Europe." *United States Army in World War I.* 2nd version. CD-ROM disc 3 of 3: 487.

Battle for Cantigny. Map. United States Army Center of Military History (2001). "American Armies and Battlefields in Europe." *United States Army in World War I.* 2nd version. CD-ROM disc 3 of 3: 415.

Battle for Sedan. Map. Based on the map illustrated in the United States Army of Military History (2001). "American Armies and Battlefields in Europe." *United States Army in World War I.* 2nd version. CD-ROM disc 3 of 3: 296.

Coffman, Edward M. *The War to End All Wars: The American Military Experience in World War I.* New York: Oxford University Press, 1968.

"Darling I Am Coming Back." Chicago Historical Society. 01 June 2009 <http://ecuip.lib.uchicago.edu/diglib/social/chi1919/aline/a1/19a1d3.html>.

Farrell, T. F. (Ed.). (1919). *A History of the 1st U.S. Engineers - 1st U.S. Division.* Coblenz, Germany.

Farrell, Thomas F. "Operations of a Divisional Engineer Regiment." *Military Engineer* (Mar/Apr 1922): 99+.

"France: St. Nazaire to Lunéville." Map. Based on the map illustrated on the Medical Department of the United States Army in the World War website: Plate I. 04 June 2009. <http://history.amedd.army.mil/booksdocs/wwi/fieldoperations/default.htm>.

Fussell, Paul. *The Great War and Modern Memory.* New York: Oxford University Press, 1975.

Lunéville Sector. Map. United States Army Center of Military History (2001). "American Armies and Battlefields in Europe." *United States Army in World War I.* 2nd version. CD-ROM disc 3 of 3: 422.

McMurray, Frank M., Ph.D., *Geography of the Great War*. MacMillan Co., NY, 1919. 22 January 2011. <http://freepages.military.rootsweb.ancestry.com/˜worldwarone/ WWI/TheGeographyOfTheGreatWar/images/Figure17-Page20.jpg>.

Meuse-Argonne Campaign—Phase 2. Map. Based on the map illustrated in the United States Army Center of Military History (2001). "American Armies and Battlefields in Europe." *United States Army in World War I*. 2nd version. CD-ROM disc 3 of 3: 226.

Meuse-Argonne Campaign—Oct. 7-10. Map. Based on the map illustrated in the United States Army Center of Military History (2001). "American Armies and Battlefields in Europe." *United States Army in World War I*. 2nd version. CD-ROM disc 3 of 3: 228.

Nelson, James Carl. *The Remains of Company D: A Story of the Great War*. New York: St. Martin's Press, 2009.

Pershing, John J. *My Experiences in the World War*. 2 vols. New York: Stokes, 1931.

"St. Mihiel 1st Division Positions." Map. Based on the map illustrated on the Medical Department of the United States Army in the World War website: Plate XXII. 04 June 2009. <http://history.amedd.army.mil/booksdocs/wwi/fieldoperations/default. htm>.

"St. Mihiel: Plan of Attack." Map. 15 January 2009. <http://www.worldwar1.com/maps/ usa523.jpg>.

"The Payday Song." *101st Airborne Songbook (1968)*. 01 June 2009 <http://www. csufresno.edu/folklore/drinkingsongs/html/books-and-manuscripts/1960s/1968-69-101st-airborne-division-songbook/index.htm> :47.

The U.S. Army in World War I, 1917-1918. 04 June 2009 <http://www.history.army.mil/ html/bookshelves/resmat/WWI.html>.

United States Army Center of Military History (2001). "The World War to May 28, 1918, and the Organization of the American Expeditionary Force." *United States Army in World War I*. 2nd version. CD-ROM, disc 3 of 3.

United States Army Center of Military History (2001). "Order of Battle of the United States Land Forces in the World War, American Expeditionary Forces: Divisions." *United States Army in World War I*, 2nd version. CD-ROM disc 3 of 3.

United States Army Center of Military History (2001). "Training and Use of American Units with the British and French." *United States Army in World War I*. 2nd version. CD-ROM disc 1 of 3.

United States Army Center of Military History (2001). "Military Operations of the American Expeditionary Forces." *United States Army in World War I*. 2nd version. CD-ROM disc 1 of 3.

United States Army Center of Military History (2001). "Policy-forming Documents of the American Expeditionary Forces." *United States Army in World War I*. 2nd version. CD-ROM disc 1 of 3.

"US Army Campaigns World War I." 01 June 2009 <http://www.history.army.mil/html/ reference/army_flag/wwi.html>.

Zone of the Army of Occupation. Map. United States Army Center of Military History (2001). "American Armies and Battlefields in Europe." *United States Army in World War I*. 2nd version. CD-ROM disc 3 of 3: 489.

Poetry Cited

Kipling, Rudyard. "Gunga Din." *Barrack-Room Ballads*, 1892.

McCrae, John. "In Flanders Fields," 1915. 14 January 2009. <http://www. arlingtoncemetery.net/flanders.htm>.

Songs of the Volunteer Army of the 1st Division. "Darling I am Coming Back." Memoirs of Charles Edward Dilkes. The Dilkes Family Papers.

Songs of the Volunteer Army of the 1st Division. "To Hell with the Engineers." Memoirs of Charles Edward Dilkes. The Dilkes Family Papers.

Southey, Robert. "After Blenheim," 1798. *The Golden Treasury of Songs and Lyrics*. The Macmillan Company. NYC, NY, 1928.

References

"155mm Schneider Howitzer." 14 January 2009. <http://www.firstdivisionmuseum.org/ museum/exhibits/tankpark/155mm.aspx>.

"Austria" or "Austria-Hungary." *The Encyclopedia Americana*, 1912 ed.

Bayly, Charles E., Gilbert Ross, Joseph Lévêque, and Ellis Slater. "History of the American Field Service in France." 21 June 2009. <http://www.lib.byu.edu/~rdh7/ wwi/memoir/AFShist/AFS2f.htm>.

"Europe, 1914." Map. *History Department at the United States Military Academy*. 21 June 2009. <http://www.dean.usma.edu/history/web03/atlases/WorldWarOne/index. htm>.

"Europe, Boundary Realignments Resulting from the War." Map. *History Department at the United States Military Academy*. 21 June 2009. <http://www.dean.usma.edu/ history/web03/atlases/WorldWarOne/index.htm>.

"Global Gazetteer Version 2.1." *World Index 2009*. 21 June 2009. <http://www. fallingrain.com/world>.

Hanlon, Michael E., editor. "The Origins of Doughboy." Doughboy Center. 16 January 2009. <http://www.worldwar1.com/dbc/origindb.htm>.

Harris, W.T., and Allen, F. Sturgis, editors. *Webster's New International Dictionary with Reference History*. G. & C. Merriam Company. Springfield, MA: Riverside Press, 1910.

Johnson, William Oscar. "In the Swim: Million-Dollar Mermaid." Article on Annette Kellerman. 16 January 2009. <http://vault.sportsillustrated.cnn.com/vault/article/magazine/MAG1068171/index.htm>.

Linder, Ann. "Feature Articles: Magical Slang: Ritual, Language and Trench Slang of the Western Front," August 2001. *First World War.Com*. 16 January 2009. <http://www.firstworldwar.com/features/slang.htm>.

Luxalbum. 2008. 16 January 2009. <http://www.luxalbum.com>.

Mead, Gary. "How the A.E.F. Dealt With: Filth, Food and Fornication." *Doughboy Center*. 14 January 2009. <http://www.worldwar1.com/dbc/mead_fff.htm>.

"Naval Architecture." *The Encyclopedia Americana*, 1912 ed.

"Propergander." Urban Dictionary Online. 2010. <http://www.urbandictionary.com/define.php?term=propergander>.

"*SS Finland*." 19 June 2009. <http://www.history.navy.mil/photos/sh-civil/civsh-f/finland.htm>.

"The Rainbow Division." August 2002. *First World War.Com*. 16 January 2009. <http://firstworldwar.com/atoz/rainbowdivision.htm>.

War Map of the French and American Front. *New Reference Atlas of the World and the War*. Rand McNally, 1918.

"World War I Victory Medal." *The Institute of Heraldry*. 15 January 2009. <http://www.tioh.hqda.pentagon.mil/Catalog/Heraldry.aspx?HeraldryId=15283&CategoryId=4&grp=4&menu=Decorations and Medals&ps=24&p=0&hilite=Victory Medal>.

INDEX

Armies

1st Army - American 109, 163, 166
1st Army - French 147
1st Battalion 38
1st Corps - American 161, 166
1st Division - American xi, xvi, 45, 71, 75, 76, 97, 105, 129, 136, 154, 156, 161, 163, 164, 165, 166, 167, 168. *See also* First Division - American
1st Engineers xvi
2nd Battalion 38
2nd Colonial Corps - French 166
2nd Division - American 105, 156, 161, 166, 167
2nd Platoon - American 95
3rd Army Corps - American 153
3rd Battalion - American 147
3rd Corps - American 166
3rd Division - American 156, 161, 166
4th Corps - American 161
4th Division - American 156, 161, 166
5th Army Corps - American 161, 164, 166, 167, 168
5th Division - American 161, 166
10th Colonial Division - French 149, 166
15th Colonial Division - French 166
15th Division - Scottish 154
17th Corps - French 166
18th Division - French 166
18th Infantry - American 147
18th Regiment - American 31, 147

19th Infantry - American 19
26th Division - American 156, 161, 166
26th Division - French 166
26th Infantry - American 72, 95, 115, 118
28th Division - American 106, 156, 166
28th Infantry - American 49, 67, 71
29th Division - American 166
32nd Army Corps - French 147, 149, 150
32nd Division - American 156, 166
33rd Division - American 166
35th Division - American 161, 166
37th Division - American 166
42nd Division - American 113, 156, 161, 166
77th Division - American 106, 166
78th Division - American 161, 166
79th Division - American 166
80th Division - American 161, 166
81st Division - American 166
82nd Division - American 161, 166
89th Division - American 161, 166, 167
90th Division - American 161, 166
91st Division - American 161, 166

A

Abainville 13, 19, 20, 21, 23
Abaucourt 118
A.E.F. 105, 128. *See also* American Expeditionary Forces
"After Blenheim" xx
Aire Valley 106

188

Aisne-Marne xii, xvi, 74, 84, 157
Algerian 35, 38, 59
Allied Armies 76, 109, 133, 136, 155, 156,
    161, 163, 170
Allies 28, 46, 76, 93, 118, 133, 134, 136, 149,
    153, 156
Alsace 33
Amarillo 23, 30
American Artillery 33, 147, 149
American Expeditionary Forces 146, 148,
    150, 151, 155, 156, 159, 160, 161, 163,
    165, 167, 168, 169. *See also* A.E.F.
American Soldiers' & Sailors' Club xi,
    128, 132
Ansauville 22, 23, 147
Antilles (transport ship) 17
Apremont 100, 149
Argonne 105, 106, 108, 109, 166
Argonne Forest 104, 108, 109, 165, 166
Arizona xxiii
Armistice xx, 113, 114, 117, 119, 126, 136
Army of Occupation 118, 123, 124
Athienville 17, 19
Austria xxiii, 41, 71, 114
Austria-Hungary xxiii, 20
Ayl 120

B

Badonvilliers 92
Bantheville 118
Bar-le-Duc 21
Barrack-Room Ballads 141
Beaumarchais 84
Beaumont-le-Sec 39
Beauvais 75
Belgium 77, 84, 128, 134
Belleau Woods 105
Berlin 103, 118, 136
Bettembourg 120
Biencourt 19, 20
Bjornstad, A.W. 153
Blenod-les-Toul 86, 91
Blue Devils 60, 84, 93
Boche 36, 38, 41, 49, 52, 53, 59, 61, 62, 64,
    65, 66, 67, 70, 71, 72, 75, 79, 80, 81,
    82, 83, 84, 87, 88, 93, 98, 100, 104,
    108, 114, 133, 147
Bois de Gouverde 19
Bois de Parois 113
Bois de Romagne 114
Bonlier 41
Bornich 121
Bourmont 12
Broyes 46
Bulgaria 113
Bullard, Maj. Gen. Robert L. 148, 150, 153

C

Cambrai 19, 36
Camp de Gerard SAS 23, 24
Camp Essayons 23, 34. *See also* Essayons
Cantigny xvi, 44, 45, 46, 50, 60, 64, 65, 66,
    67, 70, 71, 73, 136, 151
Capt. Cinquante-Cinqs 56
CFDAEF 106, 109, 110, 136, 146, 148, 149,
    150, 151, 153, 154, 155, 156, 158,
    159, 160, 161, 163, 164, 165, 167,
    168, 169, 170
Chalmaison 39
Champagne 75
Chateau-Thierry 76
Chehery 115
Chemery 115
Chepoix 45, 50
Cierges 114
Coblenz 121, 123, 125, 131
Company A 46
Company D 65
Company E xvi, 95
Company F xvi, 71
Côtes de Meuse 166
Coullemelle 67, 68, 70
Crédit Lyonnais Bank xi, 37

D

Deathman's Valley 56
Demange 20, 21
Dickman, Maj. Gen. [Joseph T.] 158
Dilkes, Charles Edward xi, xii, xiv, 141
Dilkes, Marie-Louise 128, 132. *See
    also* Marie-Louise

Discharge xi, xvi, 140
Double Traitor, The 21
Doughboys 29, 31, 51, 59, 60, 62, 64, 65,
    77, 83, 87, 108
Dudelange 120
Dutchman 60, 73

E

Eastern Front 40
Ely, Colonel [Hanson] 70
Engineers xi, xii, xvi, 3, 4, 34, 39, 45, 51,
    65, 71, 80, 91, 96, 100, 115
England 41, 130
Enlistment xi, xv, xvi
Essayons 29, 30. *See also* Camp Essayons
Etain 118
Europe xii, xviii, xxiii, 130, 144, 169
Eye xi, 5, 29, 33, 62, 77, 81, 99, 133

F

Finland (transport ship) 4, 6, 19
First Army - American 158, 160, 161, 163,
    166
First Corps - American 156
First Division - American xi, xii, xvii, 24,
    38, 100, 103, 105, 106, 109, 113, 121,
    123, 126, 129, 136, 145, 146, 147,
    148, 149, 150, 151, 155, 160, 164. *See
    also* 1st Division - American
First Engineers 4
Foch, General Ferdinand 88, 118, 160, 170
Fort Jouy 24
Fourth Corps - American 158
Fritz 49, 53, 55, 56, 57, 58, 59, 60, 61, 62,
    64, 67, 73, 76, 79, 81, 82, 83, 87, 88,
    104, 105, 108
Froissy 75

G

Garden of Elysée 132
General Order xi, 19, 78, 84, 149, 154, 156,
    158, 160, 165, 166, 169, 170
Georgetown University xi, 21
Gerauvillers 91
German National Assembly 136

Gerry 83
Gibraltar 31
Gironville 100
Givrauval 12
Golden rain 64, 99
Gondrecourt 13
Gordon Highlanders 84
"Gunga Din" 141

H

Haig, General [Sir Douglas] 159
Harreville 12
Hill 240 106
Hoboken 4, 136
Holbrook, Colonel [Lucius P.] 154
Holland 118
Hollow 30, 31, 33. *See also* Shrapnel
    Hollow
Holy Cross College xi
Huns 25, 31, 117, 133

I

Imperial Castle xxiii
"In Flanders Fields" xii, xiii
Iron Cross 98
Islettes 113
Italy xxiii, 19, 20, 40, 41, 71
Ivoiry 114

J

James, Edwin L. 136
Jersey City, New Jersey 4
Jouy-le-Grand 41
Jouy-sous-les-Côtes 23, 24, 93

K

Kaiser 118
Kane 21
Kellerman, Annette 69
King, Campbell 150, 155
Kipling, Rudyard 141
Klaxon 21, 30

L

La Gare de Paris 131
"La Marseillaise" 120
Landaville 12
Liggett, General [Hunter] 163
Ligny 21
Lincoln 153
London 136
Lookout Mountain 106
Lorraine 18, 118, 121
Lost Battalion 106
Louppy le Petit 113
Lunéville 10, 146
Luxembourg 120

M

Mabee, Colonel James I. 154
Mandres 38, 96
Manhattan Beach 18
Marchand, General 149
Marie-Louise xi, 128. *See also* Dilkes,
    Marie-Louise
Marne 79
Maron 23, 34, 38, 39
Mauvages 23
McAndrew, James W. 165
McCrae, John xii
McGlachlin, Jr., Major Gen. E.F. 133
Mesnil 62
Metz 96, 100, 161
Meuse-Argonne xvi, 102, 107, 166
Meuse River 115, 165, 166
Mexico xxiii
Montabaur 126, 130
Montdidier 42, 45, 64, 76
Montdidier-Noyon xvi
Montsec 23, 24, 28, 29, 31, 92, 93, 96
Moroccan 59
Moselle 120, 121
Mouzon 168
Mule skinners 40
Mustard gas 30

N

Naix 17
National Observer, The 141
Neufmaisons 39
Neuves-Maisons 34, 35, 36
Nogent 39
Noisy-le-Sec 39
No-man's-land 25, 27, 29, 31, 33, 64, 65, 66,
    93, 103
Nouart 117
Noyers-Saint-Martin 41, 75

O

Oelingen 120
Officers' Training Corps xvi, 21
Ormoy-villers 86

P

Pagny 41
Palmer, Lt. Col. Frederick 105
Paris xi, xii, xxiii, 17, 34, 36, 39, 42, 50, 75,
    82, 86, 118, 128, 130, 131, 132, 133
Paris Highway 80
Paris-Soissons 79
Parker, Brig. General Frank 167
Passaga, General 147, 149
Perreux-Sur-Marne 39
Persan 39
Pershing, General John J. 21, 126, 136, 139,
    151, 156, 159, 160, 161, 163, 165, 167,
    169
Pioneer Division 163
Pont-a-Mousson 87
Prussian 128, 164
Puvenelle 87

Q

Quand Même 133

R

Rainbow Division 20, 113
Rambucourt 23
Raulecourt 23, 25, 30, 95

Red Cross 80, 131
Reed, Maj. Gen. H.L. 154
Reims 93
Rhine River 125
Rocquencourt 70, 71
Roissy 76
Romagne 114
Rosieres 87, 91
Rouvres 118
Rue Royale 132
Russia xxiii, 40

S

Saint-Jean-aux-Bois 76
Saizerais 86
Salvation Army 120
Sanzey 23, 34
Sauqueuse-Saint-Lucien 75
Schrassig 120
Schwartzer 129
Sedan 115, 117, 166, 167, 168
Seraucourt 100
Serres 17, 19
Shrapnel Hollow 30. *See also* Hollow
Sibert, Wm. L. 146
Signal Corps 84
Soissons 76, 88, 91, 95, 105, 160
Sommauthe 117
Somme 40
Sommerance 114
Sommerviller 146
Sommerviller Sector 25
Sorcy 23
St. Julien 39
St. Mihiel xvi, 24, 90, 97, 101, 145, 158, 160,
    161, 166
St. Nazaire 3, 5, 7, 10, 11, 12, 19
Stonne 114, 115, 117
"Strange As It Seems" xi, 129
Strassburg 18
Summerall, Maj. Gen. Charles P. 105, 155,
    160, 164, 167, 168
Swiss 77

T

Teutonic xxiii, 40
Texas xxiii
Texas (battleship) 4, 6
Thionville 120
Third Army Corps 153, 156
Tomkinsville 4
Toul 23, 24, 38, 39, 46, 86, 147
Troyes 39, 86
Turkey 113

U

Udine 19, 41

V

Vallentigny 39
Varmaise 42, 45, 73
Vaucouleurs 91, 92
Vaudeville 5, 40, 129
Verdun 100, 103, 118, 166
Very 104
Victory Medal xvi, 73, 84, 101, 123, 152,
    157, 162, 172
Villers-Tournelle 55, 56, 62, 67, 68, 70, 71
Void 93

W

Warner, *Frau* 126
Warner, *Herr* 125, 126
Washington Barracks 3
Washington, D.C. 3, 5, 118, 159
Weimar 136
Western Front xi, xxiii, 2, 72, 109, 163, 166
Wilson, President Woodrow 159
Wirges 125
Wolmerdingen 120

Y

Y.M.C.A. 131
Ypres 83, 93